Facing the Shadow

A Guided Workbook for
Understanding and Controlling Sexual Deviance

Barbara K. Schwartz, PhD and Gregory M.S. Canfield, MSW

Illustrations incorporated by Alyce M. Kullas

Civic Research Institute, Inc.
P.O. Box 585
Kingston, NJ 08528

This workbook is intended to be used within the context of a comprehensive sex offender treatment program. Trained therapists experienced in working with sex offenders should be available to answer questions or counsel individuals completing the assignments contained herein.

Printed in the United States of America

Library of Congress Cataloging in Publication Data
Facing the shadow: a guided workbook for understanding and controlling sexual deviance/Barbara K. Schwartz and Gregory M.S. Canfield

ISBN 1-887554-01-7

Library of Congress Catalog Card Number 96-084808

INTRODUCTION

The <u>Facing the Shadow</u> workbook was developed for and has been successfully integrated into comprehensive sex offender treatment programs which include a variety of psycho-educational classes covering a broad spectrum of issues relevant to the treatment of sex offenders. The comprehensive program we suggest takes an holistic approach in which an effort is made to expose program participants to a wide variety of topics. The psycho-educational classes are part of a comprehensive treatment program which includes group work, behavioral treatment, experiential approaches and relapse prevention. More information on the Integrative Model can be found in Schwartz and Cellini (1995) <u>The Sex Offender: Corrections, Treatment and Legal Practice</u>.

One of the most effective uses of the notebook is as a reasonably non-threatening introduction to sex offender specific treatment. It is not in itself a comprehensive approach to treatment and should only be used in the context of an offense-specific sex offender treatment program.

Please address any questions you may have to:

Public Safety Concepts, Inc.
PO Box 285
North Carver, MA 02355-0285

TABLE OF CONTENTS

CHAPTER 1
LOOKING AT DEVIANCE

One out of four women will be sexually assaulted during their lifetime.
One out of six men will be sexually assaulted during their lifetime.

Sexual Assault, sexual abuse, sexual deviance, sexual addiction - these phrases fill our news broadcasts, newspapers and television talk shows. The public becomes increasingly alarmed and demands solutions - "Lock them up!" "Throw away the key!" "Castrate them!!"

You are working in this workbook because you realize that you are one of "them." However, there is something that separates you from other individuals who have problems with inappropriate sexuality. You recognize that you have a problem. Therefore, you are potentially on the road to recovery. However, this is not a smooth road. It is more like a mountain peak filled with deep crevasses, slippery rocks and loose boulders. You must be courageous, determined, and strong in order to successfully complete this journey. Mountain climbers spend countless hours in training and thousands of dollars for equipment, guides, travel, etc. What are you willing to invest?

Tears?
Sweat?
Time?
Perhaps money?

When we first began using Rob Freeman-Longo's (1988) technique of having men calculate the cost of their deviance, it was met with considerable resistance. Do you have the courage to do this?

Think briefly about what you invested in your deviance? Let's add that up?

Attorney's fees = _____

Court costs = _____

Restitution = _____

Loss of employment:
(Hourly wage x time incarcerated and estimated time finding new job)

= _____

Loss of assets:
(Home, car, tools, clothes)

= _____

Cost of deviance:
(Hourly wage x time spent involved in performing deviant acts, preparing to perform deviant acts including anytime spent with victim following first deviant impulse, time spent thinking of deviance)

= _____

Expenses associated with deviance:
(Gas, gifts for victim, meals, travel)

= _____

Expenses associated with evading capture:
(cost of giving up jobs, moving, etc.)

= _____

Total = _____

Was It Worth It?

What investment will you make in recovery? Recovery is not something you take care of once and then forget about like an appendectomy. Your problem is more like diabetes. It is something you deal with everyday. Your problem is with you everyday. It is a commitment to a total change in your lifestyle. It will involve:

- Confronting your problems head-on and solving them - not denying them, avoiding them, or skirting them
- Dealing with your emotions by experiencing them and heeding them - not medicating them, denying them, projecting them onto others.
- Analyzing your thinking by understanding how you have used distorted thinking to hurt others - not denying that you have done that.

Perhaps the most important thing you will have to do is to be honest. Be honest with yourself right now. Be honest about why you want treatment.

_____	Someone else wants me to get treatment.
_____	I like the attention I get in treatment.
_____	It's better than the alternative (e.g. going to a rougher prison).
_____	I want to get rid of my sexual deviance.
_____	I want to stop hurting others.
_____	Other reason: _____

_____

_____

There will be many times when you'll want to give up your treatment. Those impulses to leave treatment are the same impulses that will lead you back to your deviance. Think back to the last time you undermined yourself. Did you drop out of a treatment program? Did you violate probation? Did you reoffend? Perhaps it was something relatively minor such as placing yourself in a somewhat risky situation. Whatever it was, that manner of sabotaging yourself has a definite pattern. At this point, how do you feel you sabotage yourself?

_____

_____

_____

_____

_____

_____

Throughout your treatment, you will be developing your Relapse Prevention Plan by learning your pattern and how to intervene in it. You will begin to identify warning signs and high-risk situations.

You may not be in a situation right now in which you will reoffend. However, you can sabotage yourself by resisting treatment. How do you think you will do this?

(Check as many as applicable)

_____	Withdraw
_____	Get angry at my therapist
_____	Lie
_____	Blame others
_____	Manipulate others
_____	Clown around
_____	Fail to apply my therapy to my life
_____	Fail to help my fellow patients

What Is Sexual Assault?

Sexual assault is forced or tricked sexual contact which need not but can involve touching.

Sexual Assault (Check all that apply)

_____   Can happen to anyone.

_____   Is NEVER the victim's fault.

_____   Occurs without consent.

_____   Involves abuse of power.

_____   Is NEVER the product of "love" or "caring."

Sexual deviancy is a pattern of being aroused by inappropriate sexual stimuli in which there is a high probability of behaving in a sexually assaultive manner.

Sexual deviancy can involve:

Inappropriate partners

Inappropriate behaviors

Sexual relations should be positive communication of intimacy between two informed and consenting peers.

Abusive sexuality involves:

- The misuse of power and control.
- Disregard for the needs or wants of the other person.
- Using sex to express other emotions such as anger or to achieve a hidden agenda, e.g. revenge.

How were your sexual behaviors abusive? _____

_____

_____

_____

_____

_____

Look at those behaviors.   Now, how many victims have you had - not how many convictions, counts, charges - how many victims? _____

_____

_____

_____

NAME (first initial only)	AGE	HOW DID YOU SEXUALLY ABUSE THEM?
_____	_____	_____
_____	_____	_____
_____	_____	_____
_____	_____	_____
_____	_____	_____
_____	_____	_____
_____	_____	_____
_____	_____	_____
_____	_____	_____
_____	_____	_____
_____	_____	_____
_____	_____	_____
_____	_____	_____
_____	_____	_____

NAME (first initial only)	AGE	HOW DID YOU SEXUALLY ABUSE THEM?
_____	____	_____
_____	____	_____
_____	____	_____
_____	____	_____
_____	____	_____
_____	____	_____
_____	____	_____
_____	____	_____
_____	____	_____
_____	____	_____
_____	____	_____
_____	____	_____
_____	____	_____
_____	____	_____
_____	____	_____
_____	____	_____
_____	____	_____
_____	____	_____
_____	____	_____

If you have more victims than there are lines, use additional pieces of paper. Remember, sexual assault need not even involve touch. It can involve inappropriately looking at others, following them, using lewd or obscene language to shock or offend them.

Don't get into arguing about whether you penetrated your victim/s or not. The trauma of sexual assault is not based on the degree of penetration.

What About The Victims?

How many people do you know that have been sexually assaulted?

List Them:

_____

_____

_____

_____

_____

_____

_____

_____

_____

_____

_____

_____

_____

_____

_____

_____

_____

_____

_____

_____

_____

_____

Victims of sexual assault suffer lifelong effects. The girls and women are greatly over-represented among:

- Run-aways
- Substance abusers
- Prostitutes
- Mental patients
- Criminals

The men and boys are greatly over-represented among:

- Substance abusers
- Criminals

Imagine what the long and short term effects of the following types of sexual assault are?

	Short Range	Long Range

Stranger Rape:_____

_____

_____

_____

_____

_____

_____

_____

_____

_____

_____

_____

_____

                    Short Range   Long Range

Acquaintance Rape:_____

_____

_____

_____

_____

_____

_____

_____

_____

_____

_____

_____

                    Short Range   Long Range

Child Molestation by a Stranger:_____

_____

_____

_____

_____

_____

_____

_____

_____

_____

_____

_____

Short Range   Long Range

Child Molestation by an Acquaintance:_____

_____

_____

_____

_____

_____

_____

_____

_____

_____

_____

_____

_____

Short Range   Long Range

Incest:_____

_____

_____

_____

_____

_____

_____

_____

_____

_____

_____

_____

_____

A vital part of your treatment is to acknowledge what you have done to your victim. This is done by writing a Clarification Letter. This is a letter which you write to each person who has been seriously hurt by your sexually deviant behavior. **You do not, however, mail the letter.** This is part of accepting responsibility for your behavior. First decide to whom you need to write these letters - certainly your victims, but also perhaps their parents, your family, even yourself.

List Them Here:

_____

_____

_____

_____

_____

_____

_____

_____

Clarification Letter To:

Use the following formula:

Describe what you did during the sexual assault, in detail.

Describe how you set up your victim, manipulated, coerced or forced them.

Describe what you believe the consequences have been to your victim in terms of:

- Her/his emotional state
- Her/his behaviors
- Interpersonal relations
- Work/school
- Future

Never contact a victim, in any manner, unless this has been cleared with your support team, therapist, probation officer, etc. Any contact should be initiated by the victim or his/her representative.

How Did You Get Into This Mess?

First of all, the hardest belief to get rid of is: "It just happened." Very few events in this world just happen. Would you believe someone who said that suddenly they just went into a bank and robbed it? What is your response to that? _____

_____

_____

_____

_____

What if someone told you that they were just walking down the street and just happened to "hot wire" a car and steal it? What would you tell them? _____

_____

_____

_____

_____

_____

Behaviors are planned in a variety of ways. You will need to learn how you planned your sexual acting-out.

Look over the following list and honestly evaluate the types of planning you used.

_____ Carefully planned each part of the act/s.

_____ Had sexual fantasies involving your deviant behavior.

_____ Thought up reasons why this behavior was not wrong.

_____ Experienced excitement when you thought about similar behavior.

_____   Thought about how to keep from getting caught.

_____   Purchased pornography or acquired pictures of victims or

behaviors which you used to enhance your deviant fantasies.

_____   Cruised in your car or on foot looking for potential victims.

Other ways you planned your deviance: _____

_____

_____

_____

_____

It is important that you recognize how you planned your behavior because if you didn't plan your behavior, you cannot be treated. If you didn't plan your behavior, you can't be treated at all because you might do anything, anytime, anywhere.

Your Relapse Prevention Plan

Your "Relapse Prevention Plan" will be one of your most important tools of recovery. Relapse Prevention is a technique that was originally devised to help alcoholics realize that one slip-up wouldn't destroy their recovery. The model makes several assumptions:

- There is a definite series of thoughts, feelings and behaviors that lead up to deviant behavior - in this workbook, this is referred to as the "deviant cycle."
- This pattern can be identified and each step can be seen as a "warning sign."
- When people can identify their warning signs and high risk situations, they can devise ways of stopping the cycle.

Consider this scene: Joe is trying to stop smoking. He hasn't smoked for three days. He is sitting in a restaurant, having just finished a great meal. This was always his favorite time for a cigarette.

How or what do you think he is feeling?

_____

_____

_____

_____

_____

What is he thinking?

_____

_____

_____

_____

_____

What is he doing? (specific behaviors)

_____

_____

_____

_____

He might succeed in stopping the urge to smoke or he might fail. He leaves the restaurant and begins to walk down the street. He comes to a 7-11 and stands in front of the store - a store where he can buy cigarettes.

How is he feeling?

_____

_____

_____

_____

_____

What is he thinking?

_____

_____

_____

_____

_____

What are his specific behaviors?

_____

_____

_____

_____

_____

How could he stop himself from buying cigarettes?

_____

_____

_____

_____

_____

How will he feel if he can't stop himself?

_____

_____

_____

_____

_____

When would it be the easiest for him to intervene in his urge to stop smoking?

_____

_____

_____

_____

_____

Here are some definitions you should learn to help you understand Relapse Prevention.

Deviant Cycle - The pattern of specific thoughts, feelings, and behaviors which lead up to and immediately following the acting out of sexual deviance. It is often presented in this form:

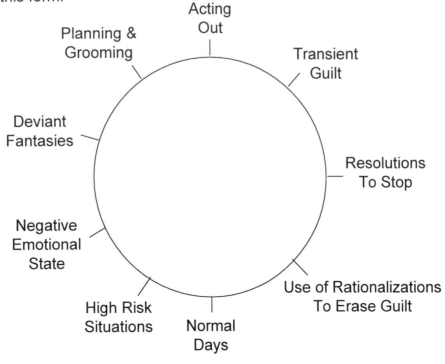

Seemingly Unimportant Decisions - Decisions which on the surface appear to have no relation to sex offending at all, but which an offender may know deep down inside will lead to high risk situations.

Abstinence Violation Effect - That feeling of hopelessness, worthlessness, and failure which you experience when you recognize that you are back in your cycle.

Lapse - Any thought, feeling, or behavior which is closely associated with a return to deviance. If a lapse is not recognized and actively dealt with, it will almost certainly be followed by a relapse but it can also serve as a useful warning sign. It is a final element in the behavior chain before reoffending which usually involves willfully initiating or remaining in very high risk situations or engaging in victimizing behavior which is just short of reoffending.

Relapse - The actual acting-out of deviance.

Acting-Out - The transforming of deviant fantasies into deviant behavior.

Fool Factor - Those unexpected events that may throw you into stress and initiate the deviant cycle.

External High Risk Situations - Circumstances which happen in the environment which can lead to negative emotional states (e.g., having a fight with a family member, being turned down for a date, being laid off).

Internal High Risk Situations - Thoughts which if dwelt on will lead to a negative emotional state (e.g., dwelling on injustices, worrying about rejection).

Recognizing Your Deviant Cycle

You may be aware of your deviant cycle at this time. You will need to carefully study your various offenses - all of them, not just those that you were caught committing. Then you will need to figure out what those acts had in common. Look at some of the factors relating to the victims.

The sex of my victims was _____

They were all between _____ and _____ years of age.

They shared the following physical characteristics: _____
_____
_____
_____

They shared the following personality characteristics: _____
_____
_____
_____

I choose them because: _____
_____
_____
_____

Look at the environment. I offended in the following physical environment (list as many as necessary): _____

_____

_____

_____

I offended between the following times: _____

_____

_____

_____

I would try to set up the following situation for the offenses: _____

_____

_____

_____

Look at your psychological condition.

Before I offended, I usually felt _____, _____,

_____, _____, _____,

_____, _____, _____,

_____, _____, _____,

I think I was feeling that way because: _____

_____

_____

_____

And I was feeling that way because: _____

_____

_____

_____

The idea is to try to work your way backwards until you can identify situations which activated your deviant cycle. You were going along, doing fine and then suddenly you were in some type of negative emotional state, feeling angry or depressed or worried or whatever and to block out that feeling, you got back into your cycle. What is your best guess at this point about what those situations were?

_____

_____

_____

_____

_____

_____

_____

_____

It is really not the situations that activated the cycle. It is what you thought of the situation. You could have had different thoughts about the situations that might have turned them from major stressors to minor annoyances.

High Risk Situation	Your Thought	What Could You Have Thought?
Woman refuses to go out or date with me.	That slut! No woman will ever want me. I'll show them.	Oh, well! She's missing a good time. I probably wouldn't have liked her anyway.

List your High Risk Situations, thoughts and alternative thoughts below:

_____   _____   _____

_____   _____   _____

_____   _____   _____

_____   _____   _____

_____   _____   _____

_____   _____   _____

_____   _____   _____

_____   _____   _____

_____   _____   _____

_____   _____   _____

Are there ways you can stay out of High Risk Situations? What are they?

_____

_____

_____

_____

_____

_____

How can you get out of High Risk Situations once you find yourself in one?

_____

_____

_____

_____

_____

_____

When you are in those situations and you begin to go into a negative emotional state, what could you do to get out of that negative emotional state?

_____

_____

_____

_____

_____

_____

The earlier in your cycle you can intervene, the better. However, you can always STOP right up to the point of actually assaulting your victim.

How can you stop those fantasies that feed you deviance?

_____

_____

_____

_____

_____

_____

_____

_____

You will learn more techniques in the next chapter.

How would you know if you were beginning to select a victim? _____

_____

_____

_____

_____

_____

_____

How could you stop yourself? _____

_____

_____

_____

_____

_____

How would you know that you were beginning to groom your victim (coaxing, intimidating, threatening, coercing, forcing)? _____

_____

_____

_____

_____

_____

_____

How could you stop yourself? _____

_____

_____

_____

_____

_____

_____

Your deviant cycle could take a few minutes to run through or it might take months. Once you let it start, you have two choices:

- You can give up control and let it take its course, as you have done in the past.
- You can take charge and stop it.

The choice is entirely up to YOU.

CHAPTER 2

YOUR PHYSICAL SELF IN RECOVERY

In this workbook you will be looking at yourself in recovery. And what is your self?

- Your physical self
- Your thinking self
- Your feeling self
- Your spiritual self
- Your self in your environment
- Your self and others

You first existed as a physical being so that facet of your being will be dealt with first. There are two ways we can look at your physical self:

- Your physical self and your deviance.
- Your physical self and your recovery.

Your body was obviously involved in your deviance. Obviously your body is involved in any behavior and therefore in any crime. However, your body is particularly involved in a sex crime.

- You were satisfying a physical need in a distorted manner.
- You were violating physical boundaries of another.
- You were converting psychological needs for anger or power or some other emotion into a physical expression.

Years ago people believed that sex crimes were committed by people who were simply "horny." They wanted sex and couldn't get it except by turning to children or resorting to violence.

Have you had appropriate sexual partners? Rate your degree of sexual satisfaction with them.

Partners   *Sexual Satisfaction (1 to 10)*

_____   _____

_____   _____

_____   _____

_____   _____

_____   _____

_____   _____

In the 1970's it was popular to say that sex crimes were not sexual - they were simply expressions of anger, power, control, etc.

If you wanted to express anger towards a woman, what would you do? List five behaviors:

_____

_____

_____

_____

_____

If you wanted to exercise power over someone, what would you do?

_____

_____

_____

_____

_____

_____

You chose sex as a means of getting those needs met. Guess why you might have done that.

_____

_____

_____

It is probably not very clear to you yet.

You use sex to satisfy a variety of needs. However, you must find that behavior or that type of victim sexually arousing. It is common for sex offenders to say that the victim was:

- A substitute for someone else.
- Chosen simply because you were drunk or on drugs.
- Assaulted because you were under stress.

However, that victim must be perceived as a sexual partner to even the drunkest person. Sometimes it is hard to admit that you are sexually aroused by violence or by children or animals or certain types of clothing, but that admission is an important step in RECOVERY.

Deviant Sexual Arousal

In order to help you identify what arouses you, your therapist may arrange to have you evaluated on a PENILE PLETHYSMOGRAPH. This is a machine which measures sexual arousal. The evaluation may work like this:

- You will go into a small private room.
- You will position yourself on a bed or a reclining chair and cover yourself with a sheet.
- You will place a small metal ring around the shaft of your penis. (This will not electrically shock you).
- You will be shown videos, slides or listen to tapes, or all three.

Just relax and let your body respond. After all, if you were sick and wanted to get well, you wouldn't want to lie about your symptoms to your doctor.

Once you know the pattern of your deviance, you can begin to learn techniques to control it and to strengthen appropriate arousal. There are several techniques you can start right now.

Start by trying not to masturbate to fantasies that involve <u>children</u> or <u>violence</u>. Each time you pair the pleasure of masturbation to thoughts about deviance, you strengthen the deviance.

In the following space, write an appropriate sexual fantasy that you would find exciting: _____

_____

_____

_____

_____

_____

_____

_____

_____

_____

_____

_____

_____

_____

_____

_____

_____

_____

Another technique you can use is called <u>Covert Sensitization</u>. This method pairs a deviant fantasy with a disgusting or frightening one. In the following space, write the beginning of one of your deviant fantasies. Describe the scene, the victim, how you are setting up the situation. Use the pronoun "I." Continue to write up to the point where you would touch the victim. Then STOP.

_____

_____

_____

_____

_____

_____

_____

_____

_____

_____

_____

_____

_____

_____

_____

In the next space, write the most disgusting scene you can produce. Remember, use "I". This is a scene of something really terrible happening to you - the more disgusting the better.

_____

_____

_____

_____

_____

_____

_____

_____

_____

_____

_____

_____

_____

_____

Now switch back to the original scene and fantasize yourself moving away from the high risk situation and being very proud of yourself. Reward yourself in the fantasy by doing something you enjoy or receiving praise from someone you admire.

_____

_____

_____

_____

_____

_____

_____

_____

_____

_____

_____

_____

_____

_____

_____

_____

_____

Now prepare a scene at least three pages long using a deviant scene paired with a disgusting one. You may begin by using the scenes you have just prepared. It is very important that the disgusting scenes make you very uncomfortable, preferably somewhat ill. You need to read these three scenes (covert script) every day for a week in a quiet, private place.

Prepare five different scripts over five weeks. Attach the scripts to this workbook. Write on each script the date and time you read it to yourself.

Other Physical Issues

The brain is the last frontier. It is not yet understood how the brain, hormones, enzymes can effect sexual behavior. There are several issues which you might want to discuss with your therapist.

Point 1 - Have you ever had any significant head injuries or an illness which caused you to be unconscious or have seizures? _____

If so, please describe: _____

_____

_____

_____

_____

_____

_____

Point 2 - Do you have trouble keeping from having deviant sexual fantasies, even when you try to stop them? Do these fantasies keep you from concentrating on other things? Do you masturbate compulsively several times a day?_____

If yes, please describe: _____

_____

_____

_____

_____

_____

Discuss this with your therapist. Medication may help.

Point 3 - Do you have problems with sexual dysfunction? Do you have problems maintaining an erection (getting a hard-on), premature ejaculation (coming too soon), or any other recondition that has made it uncomfortable, embarrassing or painful to have sex?_____

If yes, please describe: _____

_____

_____

_____

_____

Point 4 - AIDS (Acquired Immune Deficiency Syndrome) is of special concern to people in your situation. You may be in a high risk group due to your sexual habits and/or substance abuse. Have you had unprotected sex with either another male, a prostitute, a drug user or anyone you did not know well (not using a condom)? Have you shared needles when doing drugs?_____

If yes, please describe: _____

_____

_____

_____

Have you ever been tested for AIDS? A sex offender with AIDS is a murderer. Harsh words - but true. Find out your risks.

Helping Your Body Work For You

A.A. groups tell their members to watch out for HALT.   Never get too

H - Hungry

A - Angry

L - Lonely

T - Tired

These are symptoms of stress.   Avoiding stress involves changing your total LIFESTYLE so that you have lots of extra energy to deal with all those little unexpected crises.

When a person is under stress, he is spending more energy than he is receiving.

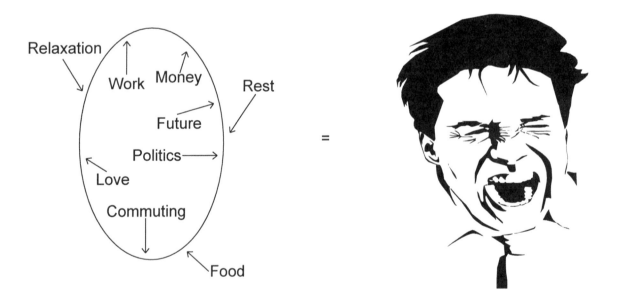

This person is worried about his work, his love life, the future, politics and commuting. He gets some energy back but not enough. He's STRESSED OUT!

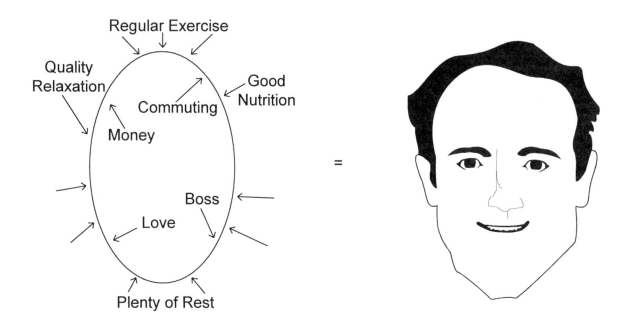

This person has concerns about money, his girlfriend, his boss and commuting but he keeps replenishing that energy with lots of good food, rest, relaxation and exercise. He's LAID BACK.

How stressed out are you? List below some of the major issues you are worried about and rate them from 1 to 10 on how much you worry about them:

_____   _____

_____   _____

_____   _____

_____   _____

_____   _____

_____   _____

_____   _____

_____   _____

_____   _____

_____   _____

List below situations which you find stressful in your current life and rate from 1 to 10 on how stressful they are:

_____   _____

_____   _____

_____   _____

_____   _____

_____   _____

_____   _____

_____   _____

_____   _____

_____   _____

In the chapter on Thinking, we will discuss some ways of dealing with worries. Here we will discuss ways in which you can supply your body with more energy.

Nutrition

Your eating habits can save your life or literally kill you. Evaluate your eating habits using the following scale:

(0) Never   (1) Seldom   (2) Occasionally   (3) Frequently   (4) Always

Use foods to reward yourself or to punish yourself.   _____

Eat when you are not hungry.   _____

Rush through meals.   _____

Eat when upset.   _____

Think about dieting.   _____

Sneak food. _____

Prefer to eat alone. _____

Go on "binges" where you eat a great deal in a short period of time. _____

Skip breakfast or eat junk food for breakfast. _____

Eat to the point of being stuffed. _____

Vomit or use laxatives to keep from gaining weight. _____

Eat junk food shortly before retiring. _____

SCORE:

Under 10	-	Congratulations!
10 - 16	-	You are a sensible eater.
17 - 24	-	Some improvement needed.
25 - 35	-	Much improvement needed.
Over 35	-	You have to make serious changes.

In the next section, write down what you have eaten in the last two days. (Include all beverages).

DAY 1   BREAKFAST   DAY 2

_____   _____

_____   _____

_____   _____

_____   _____

DAY 1   LUNCH   DAY 2

_____   _____

_____   _____

_____   _____

_____   _____

_____   _____

DAY 1	DINNER	DAY 2
_____		_____
_____		_____
_____		_____
_____		_____
_____		_____

DAY 1	SNACKS	DAY 2
_____		_____
_____		_____
_____		_____
_____		_____

Cups of Coffee   _____   _____

Now evaluate your diet.

Check off:

- Simple sugars - cakes, donuts, cookies, etc. but also ketchup, non-dairy coffee creamers, prepared salad dressing - these represent calories without nutrition.

- Fats - red meats and whole (not skim or low-fat) milk products - these contribute to heart attacks and strokes.

Are you eating fish, chicken, whole grains, vegetables, fresh fruit? Even if you are in an institution, you can improve your diet.

Make a list of foods you have purchased in the last two weeks. For each purchase consider a healthier alternative including non-food items:

<table>
<tr><td><u>Purchase</u></td><td><u>Healthier Substitute</u></td></tr>
<tr><td><u>Candy bars</u></td><td><u>Magazines</u></td></tr>
<tr><td><u>Sodas</u></td><td><u>Bottled Water</u></td></tr>
</table>

Watch your intake of caffeine - latest studies suggest that more than four cups of coffee a day can be bad for you.

Exercise That Take Stress Away

People often say that they are too tired to exercise. Actually exercise can

- combat fatigue.

- make you feel energized.

- build up your physical resources so you can cope with stress better.

What types of exercise do you engage in now?

_____

_____

_____

_____

A good exercise program should:

- Lower your resting heart rate.

- Raise your training heart rate.

- Speed up your recovery heart rate.

Evaluate your exercise:

- Check your resting heart rate by finding the pulse in your wrist and counting the beats in one minute (it should be less than 70 beats per minute). What is yours? _____ A good exercise program will lower it.

- Check your training heart rate (it should be 70 percent of your maximum heart rate). Start with 220 and subtract your age. Now multiply this figure by .70. This is your training heart rate. Exercise at this rate for 20 minutes four times a week. Training heart rate = _____.

- Check your recovery heart rate. Reach your training heart rate - stop. Wait one minute. Your heart rate should drop at least 25 beats. It will drop more as you get fitter. Time it takes to drop 25 beats _____.

(Ardell and Tager, 1982)

Exercise can be a real chore or the best part of your day. The trick is finding something you enjoy.

What exercise sport or exercise can you do now that you enjoy?

_____

_____

_____

_____

In the best of worlds with all the time, money, and freedom you need, what exercise sport or exercise would you enjoy?

_____

_____

_____

_____

Have any of these exercise, sports, or activities that are associated with your deviance? Jogging to cruise for victims? Walking through playgrounds? Discuss what activities you need to stay away from. _____

_____

_____

_____

_____

Now be realistic! What activities can/will you actually do. Evaluate these activities:

ACTIVITIES	I can afford to do this (daily, weekly, monthly, yearly)	It is available (daily weekly, monthly, yearly)	It avoids high-risk situations (yes/no)
_____	_____	_____	_____
_____	_____	_____	_____
_____	_____	_____	_____
_____	_____	_____	_____
_____	_____	_____	_____
_____	_____	_____	_____
_____	_____	_____	_____
_____	_____	_____	_____
_____	_____	_____	_____
_____	_____	_____	_____
_____	_____	_____	_____

You have seen how your physical needs are involved in your deviance and how taking care of yourself physically can give you the energy to support recovery. However, you must not allow yourself to believe that your body is the source of your deviance. You did not sexually assault someone because you had to satisfy your sexual urges. The reason you engaged in sexual deviance had to do with your

thoughts

and

feelings.

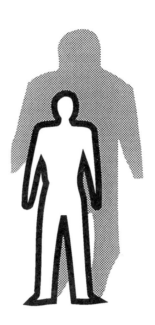

CHAPTER 3

YOUR COGNITIVE SELF IN RECOVERY

What is your cognitive self? Your cognitive self has to do with your thoughts, your "thinking" self.

Your thoughts can

- Produce emotions
- Justify your deviance
- Rationalize your behaviors

Hopefully one uses one's mind to solve problems.
One is advised to

- Use your head
- Think about it

However, you may or may not know how to solve your problems by "thinking about them." If you don't know how to

- Effectively problem solve
- Identify distorted thoughts

you may make your problems worse, depending on how you THINK ABOUT IT.

You can strengthen or weaken your sexual arousal by how you think about it. You have already seen how you can use thoughts in <u>covert sensitization</u> to decrease your arousal.

Some people are bothered by recurrent, intrusive thoughts which seem to have a life of their own - they pop into your mind frequently despite your efforts to suppress them.

What Should You Do About Them?

- Don't try to suppress them because they may gain in strength.
- Simply note them and shift your thoughts to something pleasant and positive.

Your "Stinkin' Thinking"

Think back to when you were offending. What thoughts did you use to keep your deviant behavior going? _____

_____

_____

_____

_____

Certain thoughts specifically kept your deviance going. However, "stinkin' thinkin'" may have caused a number of problems in your life. Two therapists, Dr.'s Yockelson and Samenow, came up with a theory about how people's thoughts get them in trouble. They referred to this process as "criminal thinking." However, not all "criminals" show all these errors while plenty of people who aren't "criminals" show these patterns. Thus in this workbook these thinking errors will be referred to as "stinkin' thinkin'." Now look at some of the ways you may use these thought patterns. Give an example of how you or someone you know may have engaged in "stinkin' thinkin'." Describe the situation and the thought.

VICTIM STANCE: ("She made me do it." "It's his fault." "If she hadn't, I wouldn't have had to.") _____

_____

_____

_____

I CAN'T: ("I can't do that." "I could never do that.") _____

_____

_____

_____

_____

INABILITY TO UNDERSTAND INJURY TO OTHERS: ("I didn't hurt her/him." "What I did has had no long range effect). _____

_____

_____

_____

_____

FAILURE TO EMPATHIZE WITH OTHERS: ("She/he deserved it." "All women/men are jerks/sluts/creeps.") _____

_____

_____

_____

_____

LACK OF EFFORT: ("It's too hard/difficult/much trouble." "I'm not up to it because I'm sick/dumb/tired/upset." _____

_____

_____

_____

_____

REFUSAL TO ACCEPT OBLIGATIONS: ("I forgot." "It's not my problem/responsibility." "I'll do what I want - not what's right.") _____

_____

_____

_____

_____

LACK OF TRUST: ("Everyone's out to get me." "I can't trust you.") _____

_____

_____

_____

_____

UNREALISTIC EXPECTATIONS: ("It will work out because I think it will." "Others will do what I want.") _____

_____

_____

_____

_____

IRRESPONSIBLE DECISION MAKING: ("I don't need to worry about facts." "Things will work out the way I planned it.") _____

_____

_____

_____

_____

PRIDE: ("You'll never make me change my mind." "I'm right regardless.") _____

_____

_____

_____

_____

REFUSAL TO ACKNOWLEDGE FEAR: ("I'm not afraid of anything." "Only punks are afraid.") _____

_____

_____

_____

_____

MISUNDERSTANDING ANGER: ("I don't get mad - I get even." "I can't control my anger." "Don't get me mad or it'll be your fault when I act-out.") _____

_____

_____

_____

_____

POWER TACTICS: ("I must be in control" "I've got to be on top or I'll be on the bottom.) _____

_____

_____

_____

_____

PERFECTIONISM: ("It's all right - or all wrong." "You made a mistake and I'm going to punish you.") _____

_____

_____

_____

_____

SECRECY: ("What they don't know, won't hurt them." "They don't need to know about that.") _____

_____

_____

_____

_____

LYING: ("I'll never admit to that." "It will be easier to talk about if I change it - just a little.") _____

_____

_____

_____

_____

OVER-RATED OPINION OF SELF: ("I'm really a good person - just misunderstood." "I just made a mistake - anyone can make a mistake.") _____

_____

_____

_____

_____

You can change your life by changing the way you think.

- Thinking patterns can be recognized and changed.

- Different people have different types of thinking patterns.

- Behaviors are the result of thoughts.

A Pattern of Antisocial Thinking

Dr. Jack Bush of the Vermont Department of Corrections has devised a chart to show how <u>antisocial thinking</u> works.

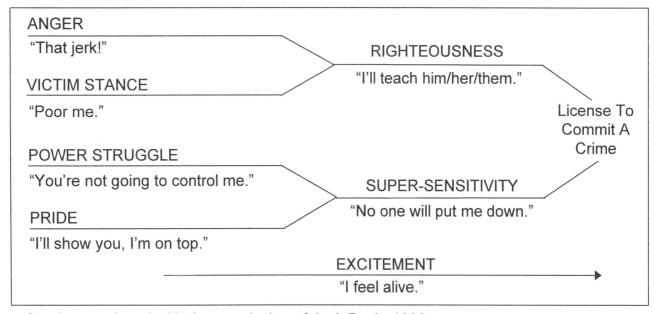

ANGER
"That jerk!"

VICTIM STANCE
"Poor me."

RIGHTEOUSNESS
"I'll teach him/her/them."

License To Commit A Crime

POWER STRUGGLE
"You're not going to control me."

PRIDE
"I'll show you, I'm on top."

SUPER-SENSITIVITY
"No one will put me down."

EXCITEMENT
"I feel alive."

Graph reproduced with the permission of Jack Bush, 1996.

How might a sex offender combine these thought patterns to justify committing a sexual assault?

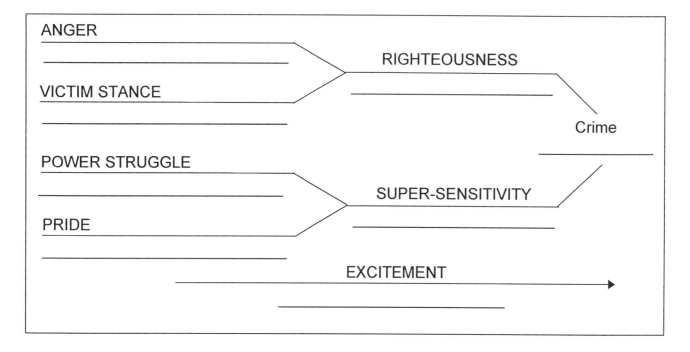

The Con Code

People in prison develop certain ways of thinking to make themselves feel better about their situation.

Rules of the "Con Code" include:

- Don't trust
- Don't feel
- Don't talk

TRUST: "It's us versus them." (C.O.'s, shrinks, teachers in prison, nurses in prison, counselors.)

FEELING: "Don't let them know they've gotten to you." "Don't let them see your weaknesses."

TALKING: "Do your own time."

Give some examples of the "Con Code."

_____

_____

_____

_____

_____

_____

_____

_____

_____

Following the "Con Code" means:

Loyalty - to the Con Code

Self-sufficiency

Pride

Dominating others or being dominated

Power (or weakness)

Feeling proud (or feeling belittled)

Hurting others (or being hurt)

Looking down on others (or being looked down on)

Suspicion (or being suspected)

Hey buddy, listen up. This is the way it is around here. Ya got it?

What type of person does this set of beliefs produce? _____

_____

_____

_____

_____

_____

_____

Against the "Con Code" stands

THE RECOVERY CODE

TRUST	COOPERATION
FEEL	TRUST
TALK	GENTLENESS
RESPECT	LOVE
CONSIDERATION	

You will need to constantly keep track of your thoughts to stay in the Recovery Code.

Your assignment is to:

- Keep a journal of your "Con Code" thoughts each day for a week.

- Write down the thought, the time, the situation.

- Write down a RECOVERY CODE response to the situation.

Attach your journal to this workbook.

Improving Your Problem-Solving Skills

There are four kinds of people in this world.

Smart-Smart People

Smart-Stupid People

Stupid-Smart People

Stupid-Stupid People

Smart-smart people have the basic skills and use them in an intelligent way.

Smart-stupid people have the basic skills but don't know how to use them.

Stupid-smart people don't have the basic skills but may have sense about problem-solving and know what skills they need to acquire.

Stupid-stupid people don't have the skills and can't problem-solve. They don't know and don't know that they don't know.

You can be a smart-smart person in some situations and a stupid-stupid or smart-stupid or stupid-smart person in another.

Sex offenders tend to have trouble solving problems when they are under certain types of stresses, e.g. feeling rejected, powerless, angry, etc.

However, You Can Learn To Think More Effectively.

Step 1 - Recognize a problem exists

Step 2 - Identify the real problem

Step 3 - Get the facts

Step 4 - Consult with people you respect

Step 5 - Consider all the alternatives

Step 6 - Consider all the consequences

Step 7 - Pick the best solution for you

Step 8 - Check out how it is working

Choose a situation in your life where you had a problem and did not handle it well. Describe the situation: _____

_____

_____

_____

_____

Step 1 - Recognize the problem. (How should you have known you had a problem? List all the cues you can now see). _____

_____

_____

_____

_____

_____

_____

_____

_____

_____

Step 2 - Identify the real problem. (What was the real problem and what should have been the goal?) _____

_____

_____

_____

_____

_____

_____

_____

_____

Step 3 - Get the facts. (Were there facts which you failed to take account of that should have been considered?) _____

_____

_____

_____

_____

_____

_____

_____

_____

Step 4 - Consult with people you respect. (What would they have advised you?) _____

_____

_____

_____

_____

_____

_____

_____

Step 5 - Consider all the alternatives. (What would have been alternatives?)_____

_____

_____

_____

_____

_____

_____

_____

_____

Step 6 - Consider all the consequences. (Outline the pros and cons for each alternative.)

	Pros	Cons
Alternative #1	_____	_____
	_____	_____
	_____	_____
	_____	_____
	_____	_____
	_____	_____

	Pros	Cons
Alternative #2	_____	_____
	_____	_____
	_____	_____
	_____	_____
	_____	_____
	_____	_____

	Pros	Cons
Alternative #3	_____	_____
	_____	_____
	_____	_____
	_____	_____
	_____	_____

	Pros	Cons
Alternative #4	_____	_____
	_____	_____
	_____	_____
	_____	_____
	_____	_____

Step 7 - Pick the best solution for you. (Why did you make that choice?)_____

_____

_____

_____

_____

_____

_____

_____

_____

Step 8 - Check it out. (How do you think that solution would have worked?) _____

_____

_____

_____

_____

_____

_____

_____

How did your actual solution work? _____

_____

_____

_____

_____

_____

_____

Let's look at some more problem-solving activities. Many of these techniques were taken from a program called <u>Deciding</u> by H.B. Gelatt, B.B. Varenhorst, and R. Carey. These authors point out that there are three requirements of skilled decision-making:

- Knowing your personal values
- Knowing and using relevant information
- Knowing and using effective strategy for converting information into action

Values - an abstract quality which someone prizes, cherishes and esteems and expresses consistently in his behavior. These may be issues like:

Power	Respect	Individuality
Wealth	Family	Prestige
Fame	Love	Conformity
Success	Friendship	Hard work
Honesty	Security	Religion
Obedience	Happiness	Comfort
Freedom	Solitude	Approval
	Others	

Think about choices you have made in your life. What values do you think it reflected?

CHOICE   I Thought It Would Get Me

                                (List as many as appropriate)

_____   _____

_____   _____

_____   _____

_____   _____

_____   _____

_____   _____

_____   _____

_____   _____

Can you see a pattern? If you are to be happy with your decision, they must reflect your values.

What are these values - be honest - don't second guess what you think "the best values" are.

1. _____

2. _____

3. _____

4. _____

Information - you will need information on:

- Possible alternative actions
- Possible outcomes
- Probability of various outcomes
- Desirability of outcomes

Pretend that you are totally free to choose where to live. List (5) places that appeal to you.

1. _____
2. _____
3. _____
4. _____
5. _____

Now you must gather some information so that you can weigh the PROS and CONS. Actually gather information. List your sources of information.

_____
_____
_____
_____
_____

Compile your information.

	PROS	CONS
PLACE 1	_____	_____
	_____	_____
	_____	_____
	_____	_____
	_____	_____
PLACE 2	_____	_____
	_____	_____
	_____	_____
	_____	_____

PLACE 3

_____   _____

_____   _____

_____   _____

_____   _____

PLACE 4

_____   _____

_____   _____

_____   _____

_____   _____

PLACE 5

_____   _____

_____   _____

_____   _____

Now go back to the list of Pros and Cons and star (*) the most important ones. You may discover that some places have extremely attractive PROS while others have very definite CONS.

It would be very easy if one place had all the PROS and the rest all the CONS. However, that is probably not the way it has worked out.

Your choice will now depend on how much of a risk-taker you are. There are four strategies one can now choose from:

WISH STRATEGY -   The alternative that could lead to the most desirable result, regardless of risk.

ESCAPE STRATEGY -   The alternative that is most likely to award the worst possible result.

SAFE STRATEGY -   The alternative that is most is likely to bring success, the highest probability.

COMBINATION STRATEGY -   The alternative that has the high probability and high desirability.

(Gelatt et al, 1972)

Let's say you are an aspiring actor and you are moving to a place to pursue your acting career. Your primary goal is a career in the theater.

WISH -   You might move to New York City because you could become a Broadway star.

ESCAPE -   You might choose Podunk, Idaho because you could probably always get a part in their Community Theater - even though it's totally amateur, at least you wouldn't fail by being unable to get any part.

SAFE -   You might choose Seattle because it has more theaters per person than anywhere else and therefore there are lots of parts although few paying ones.

COMBINATION -   You might choose San Francisco where there is prestige theater but not quite as much competition as New York.

What do you want most out of the place you live?_____

_____

_____

Where could you certainly achieve that regardless of the risk?_____

_____

Where would you have the best chance of gaining something close to what you want?

_____

Where would you have the greatest chance of gaining the highest quality of what you want?_____

There are other strategies that people use:

IMPULSIVE -   Little thought, just acting without considering alternatives.

FATALISTIC -   Letting the environment decide.

COMPLIANT -   Let someone else decide.

PLANNING -   Rational approach, balance thoughts and feelings.

INTUITIVE -   Let feelings dictate decision.

PARALYSIS -   Afraid of deciding.

(Gelatt et al, 1972)

What kind of decision - making process led you to sexually assaulting someone?

_____

_____

_____

_____

_____

_____

_____

_____

_____

_____

_____

_____

_____

_____

_____

You will have to learn how to make good decisions in all aspects of your life if you are going to avoid the stress that could contribute to your sexual deviance.

CHAPTER 4

YOUR FEELINGS IN RECOVERY

Some experts on human behavior say that "THOUGHTS PRODUCE FEELINGS. Others say "FEELINGS PRODUCE THOUGHTS". Whichever way is true - both contribute to your perception of the world - both contribute to your **sexual deviance.**

People can choose a variety of ways to deal with emotions.

     * They may over-react to all their emotions.

     * They can experience some emotions but refuse to acknowledge others.

     * They can refuse to acknowledge any emotions.

     * They can experience their emotions, understand them and integrate
       them into their lives.

How have you dealt with your emotions? (Be extra honest with yourself)

_____

_____

_____

_____

Our emotions are like a rainbow over our lives - some of the colors are cheerful, bright, sparkling - others are dark and somber. Without emotions one's life is lived in Black and White.

Another way to thing about emotions is to think of a **piano**.

A person who can experience all of his emotions plays the music of his life on a full keyboard. However, the more one is emotionally blocked, the fewer keys are used.

Society and families influence which emotions one is most comfortable experiencing.   Which emotions do you think women are most comfortable feeling?_____

_____

_____

Which emotions do you think men are most comfortable feeling?_____

_____

_____

Families allow their members to have various emotions. Which emotions did your family:

Forbid   Allow

_____   _____

_____   _____

_____   _____

_____   _____

_____   _____

Was it different for males than for females? (If so, how?)_____

_____

_____

How many emotions do you now or have you experienced?   Draw how that emotion feels.

POSITIVE FEELINGS   **NEGATIVE FEELINGS**

_____ Happy _____   _____ Sad _____

71

_____ ◯   _____ ◯

_____ ◯   _____ ◯

_____ ◯   _____ ◯

_____ ◯   _____ ◯

_____ ◯   _____ ◯

_____ ◯   _____ ◯

EXPLORING SOME EMOTIONS

List the five (5) emotions that you experience most frequently.

1._____

2._____

3._____

4._____

5._____

* When did you first experience this emotion and what were the circumstances?

_____

_____

_____

_____

* When did you most strongly experience this emotion?

_____

_____

_____

_____

* How do you usually show this emotion?

_____

_____

_____

_____

* When was the last time you had this emotion?

_____

_____

_____

_____

CUTTING OFF EMOTIONS

Have you ever stopped having an emotion? Sometimes it is just too painful to experience an emotion and one simply resolves not to experience it anymore.

List emotions you have "cut off".

1._____

2._____

3._____

4._____

5._____

Answer these questions (on extra pages) for each:

* Why did you cut off that emotion?

* Describe the circumstance in detail.

* How old were you?

CAMOUFLAGING EMOTIONS

Some people respond to some emotions by changing them into other emotions. Are you aware that you may turn emotions into anger? This is known as camouflaging.

List the emotions you camouflage.

1. I experience_____as_____

2. I experience_____as_____

3. I experience_____as_____

4. I experience_____as_____

5. I experience_____as_____

SHAME: A COMPLEX EMOTION

Motivation to hurt others may come from the way one feels about oneself.

* People who feel good about themselves rarely hurt others.

* People who feel appropriate guilt and shame after they hurt someone make an effort not to hurt others in the future.

* HOWEVER, people who experience what John Bradshaw calls "toxic shame" often end up hurting themselves and others again and again.

Toxic Shame - "is experienced as the all-pervasive sense that I am flawed and defective as a human being." (Bradshaw, 1988)

Toxic Shame is like acid being dropped on the self.

It eats part of the self away and it keeps eating until it is neutralized.

People want to cover up the hole so that neither themselves or others will notice it - so they stuff the hole full of something to cover it up. Usually compulsive behavior fills that void. This behavior becomes the bloodied, pus-filled packing that hides the wound from the world and from yourself.

COMPULSIVE BEHAVIOR - sex, drugs, alcohol, eating, working, gambling, spending.

But because the healing air and appropriate medicine can't reach the wound, it continues to fester, to cause pain and to get bigger. More packing is stuffed into it.

With treatment one pulls out all that packing and lets openness bring healing.

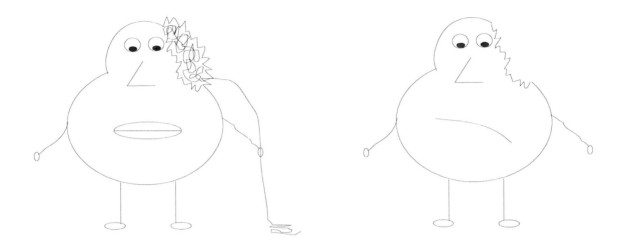

It's painful and embarrassing to reveal the wound but it must be done. No speck of the wound must be left covered or it will continue to infect the wound.

Let in the light - uncover the pain.

WHERE DID THE WOUND COME FROM?

Toxic shame comes from:

> Families
>
> Abandonment
>
> Neglect
>
> Abuse
>
> Physical
>
> Sexual
>
> Emotional
>
> School Peers
>
> Ridicule
>
> Labeling
>
> Society
>
> Prejudice
>
> Poverty
>
> and many other sources.

Sexual deviance can mask the pain of toxic shame by producing a mood-altering experience that distracts. However, it then enhances the shame and from there the addictive cycle begins.

What does shame feel like to you?

_____   _____

_____   _____

_____   _____

_____   _____

_____   _____

Can you think of sources of shame in your own life?

_____   _____

_____   _____

_____   _____

_____   _____

_____   _____

Shame can combine with other emotions. (Bradshaw calls these "Shame Parfaits")

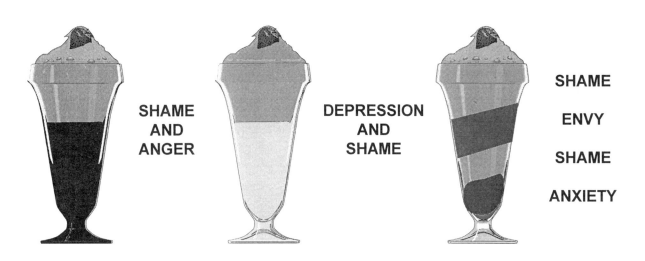

**SHAME
AND
ANGER**

**DEPRESSION
AND
SHAME**

SHAME

ENVY

SHAME

ANXIETY

In your case shame may have combined with anger or another emotion that made you want to

LASH OUT

against others.

Even if you have fooled yourself into believing that you acted out of

Love

Friendship

Caring

You hurt others and caused them

SHAME.

SEXUAL ABUSE - A SPECIAL KIND OF SHAME

There are a variety of different types of sexual abuse - however, all produce toxic shame.

Sexual abuse includes:

* Physical sexual abuse - hands-on touching in a sexual way, including rape.
* Overt sexual abuse - voyeurism or exhibitionism including watching the child or displaying one's self to the child in a way that is sexually stimulating to the adult.

John Bradshaw (1989) used the following categories.

* Covert sexual abuse
* Verbal - inappropriate sexual talking
* Boundary violation - children witnessing sexual activity.
* Emotional sexual abuse - cross-generational bonding when parent uses child to meet emotional need.

Which have you committed on others? Honestly evaluate your behaviors.

_____

_____

_____

_____

_____

_____

Were you victimized in one or more of these ways during your childhood?

_____

_____

_____

_____

_____

Patrick Carnes (1989) points out that sexually victimized children experience the following traumas.

* End up not trusting adults.

* Believe the sexual abuse is their fault.

* Are forced to keep the abuse secret which adds to shame.

* If harmed physically, equate pain with sex.

* Feel powerless.

* Associate sex with being degraded and losing self respect.

* Feel they aren't in control of their bodies.

* Confuse sex with intimacy and love.

(Carnes, 1989)

Looking at the above list, what are your feelings?

_____

_____

_____

_____

_____

HEALING THE PAIN

Step 1: The first step in healing is to acknowledge the hidden shame of pain in your past. The Adult Children Movement has brought past pain and abuse out in the open for many people. These people are viewing themselves as survivors and actively seeking

RECOVERY

rather than hiding in

SHAME.

What are some childhood pains that you need to deal with?

_____

_____

_____

_____

_____

You will need to find a therapeutic environment in which to deal with these issues. If you are currently in treatment, make sure you bring up these issues. If not, seek a therapist and a support group.

Step 2: Coping with problems often means first gaining an intellectual understanding of them. There are numerous books, workbooks, audio tapes and magazine articles on topics related to families, abuse, addiction, etc.

Make a list here of books, articles, etc. That you intend to read to help you understand this situation.

_____

_____

_____

_____

_____

_____

_____

_____

Step 3: This is probably the most painful stage as it is the part of recovery that involves getting in touch with the pain that has been locked up within you. Many therapists talk about getting in touch with the "Inner Child".

* The "Inner Child" is a way of thinking about those very painful feelings which originated in childhood trauma and are still being held within.
* Your therapist and group will help you relive some of those old feelings.
* If you begin to remember some of these old traumas outside of a therapeutic experience, write down your memories, making drawings if you are comfortable expressing yourself through art, talk to someone you trust.

Step 4: Recognize how your past is driving your present. Are there old messages, inner voices, behaviors which came from your childhood and are still controlling yours?

* Do you do things that you saw your parent(s) do and swore you would never do?

_____

_____

_____

_____

_____

* Do you tell yourself negative things that your parent(s) used to tell you?

_____

_____

_____

_____

_____

* Do you have memories that continue to influence your behavior? (E.g. I'll never cry like that again. I'll never let someone treat me like that again.)

_____

_____

_____

_____

_____

Step 5: You will begin to disengage from the trauma of your past. This may mean establishing a different relationship with your family. It may mean getting untangled from old relationships.

Do you have any idea today of the people that you have unfinished business with?

_____

_____

_____

_____

_____

_____

_____

EVERY CHILD IS ENTITLED TO CERTAIN RIGHTS

* The right to be the object of unconditional parental love.

* The right, for a time, to be the center of parental attention and have needs met without request.

* The right for consistency, limits, security, warmth and understanding.

* The right to be loved for what he or she is rather than for being what others wish him / her to be or become.

* The right to be parented and nurtured rather than falling under the enormous weight of making up for the losses of her / his parents.

* The right to be protected from traumatic situations and stresses.

(Middleton-Moz and Dwinnell, 1986)

However, if one is deprived of those rights, it does not give him / her the right to take their anger out on others.

LOOKING AT YOUR ABUSE

In thinking back on your experiences with shame, you may realize that you were

* Psychologically abused

* Physically abused

* Sexually abused

Some people who sexually abuse others have been abused - others have not. Some people choose to lie about being abused or exaggerate this in order to gain sympathy from others. If one does this - it only hurts your own search.

What is Real?

Many people are remembering early abuse of which they previously had no recollection. Many of these memories are completely true. Some of these memories are not at all true.

If most of your group members report having been sexually abused, you may come to believe that since you too are an offender that you must have been abused also. This is not necessarily the case. Many sex offenders were not abused.

To help you understand what is real you might want to contact people from your past who were familiar with your situation. Sometimes family members are too frightened by emerging memories to provide clarification. You might want to get school records, medical or other reliable records that may be available to you. When you review these records, look for any dramatic changes in your behavior that the records may show. Review the details of your own memories. Below are some questions you can ask yourself:

1. Could you have been in the place you remember?

2. Were you around the person who you recall abusing you at that time in your life?

3. Was your attendance in school interrupted?

4. Was there any remarkable medical involvement at that time?

5. Could you find any documentation of your behavior changing around that time? Grades? Conduct?

Be particularly suspicious of memories which involve bizarre activities, ritualistic abuse or memories which get worse over time.

Always share your concerns with your treatment group.

If you know that you were abused, continue through this section. If you weren't, skip this section.

<u>Psychological abuse</u>

Your age	Abuser	Description of abuse
_____	_____	_____
		_____
		_____
_____	_____	_____
		_____
		_____
		_____
_____	_____	_____
		_____
		_____
		_____
_____	_____	_____
		_____
		_____

How did it make you feel?_____

_____

_____

How did you deal with it?_____

_____

_____

How do you deal with it now?_____

_____

_____

<u>Physical abuse</u>

Your age	Abuser	Description of abuse
_____	_____	_____
		_____
		_____
_____	_____	_____
		_____
		_____
_____	_____	_____
		_____
		_____
_____	_____	_____
		_____
		_____

How did it make you feel?_____

_____

_____

How did you deal with it?_____

_____

_____

How do you deal with it now?_____

_____

_____

<u>Sexual abuse</u>

Your age	Abuser	Description of abuse
_____	_____	_____
		_____
		_____
_____	_____	_____
		_____
		_____
_____	_____	_____
		_____
		_____
_____	_____	_____
		_____
		_____

How did it make you feel?_____

_____

_____

How did you deal with it?_____

_____

_____

How do you deal with it now?_____

_____

_____

Many people have been abused but they do not abuse others. Why do you think you chose to abuse others rather than remembering how it felt when you were being abused?

_____

_____

_____

_____

_____

LOOKING AT YOUR ANGER

Anger is probably one of the emotions you have had trouble with. Which ways do you use to handle emotion?

(Check all that are applicable)

_____ Stuff it

_____ Ignore it until you explode

_____ Scream and yell

_____ Throw things

_____ Use physical violence

_____ Use sarcasm

_____ Plot revenge

_____ Other _____

_____

_____

Have you found positive ways of handling anger? What are they?_____

_____

_____

_____

_____

WHAT MAKES YOU ANGRY?

List five (5) incidents when you became extremely angry.

1. _____

_____

2. _____

_____

3. _____

_____

4. _____

_____

5. _____

_____

How do others "make" you angry?_____

_____

_____

_____

_____

Other people can not really make you angry because you must first give them that power over you.

How would you respond to these situations?

A stranger comes up to you and yells, "You, jerk! Get out of my way before I deck you!!"

1. The stranger is your age, sober, male and appears to be angry but otherwise normal.

   Are you angry?_____
   What do you think?_____

   _____

What do you do?_____

_____

2. The stranger is a 70 year old "bag lady".

   Are you angry?_____

   What do you think?_____

_____

   What do you do?_____

_____

3. The stranger is a mentally retarded man.

   Are you angry?_____

   What do you think?_____

_____

   What do you do?_____

_____

Were you mad at some of these people but not others?_____

What made this difference?_____

_____

_____

_____

_____

_____

Did you notice that you defined the situation differently for the various strangers? You had certain thoughts which defused the situation.

Your thoughts and perceptions will determine your emotion. They will defuse or escalate your reaction.

Describe the last time you were very angry._____

_____

_____

_____

What thoughts would have made the situation worse?_____

_____

_____

_____

What thoughts might have defused the situation?_____

_____

_____

_____

Keep an Anger Log for one week.

Use the following format.

Date	Situation	How you perceived the situation in a way that made you angry.	Give three (3) alternatives ways of perceiving the situation that could have reduced your anger.

Can you think of some thoughts that you can teach yourself to use to hold off anger when you first feel it?

1. _____

_____

2. _____

_____

3. _____

_____

POSITIVE EMOTIONS

People who cut off their emotions so they won't feel bad also end up cutting off emotions that would make them feel good. Therefore they find artificial ways to make themselves feel good including:

- Alcohol
- Drugs
- Gambling
- Buying
- Sex
- What others might one use

_____

_____

_____

Usually these are used in excess because they are being used in desperation to replace real

      * Happiness

      * Joy

      * Contentment

      * Excitement

THE EMOTIONAL RELAPSE PATTERN

As part of the cycle of sexual abuse, your emotions changed in a patterned manner.

What emotion do you feel as an initial warning that you are getting into cycle?

_____

_____

_____

_____

_____

How do your emotions change as you get ready to commit the sexual assault?

_____

_____

_____

_____

_____

_____

_____

How could you deal with these emotions at each stage to defuse them?

EMOTION   **RESPONSE**

_____   _____

                            _____

                            _____

_____   _____

                            _____

                            _____

_____   _____

                            _____

                            _____

_____   _____

_____   _____

_____   _____

Throughout your therapy you will have to deal with emotions.

* Emotions from your past that you have denied.

* Emotions such as guilt which are connected with your crimes.

* Emotions that you feel for others around you.

* Emotions connected with fear of the future.

Many of these emotions may be very painful. One may be tempted to ignore or deny them. BUT THEY WON'T GO AWAY! They have been effecting one's life whether one knows it or not. They will go on effecting one's life if you choose to ignore them.

Handle them now and you will
experience tremendous relief.

CHAPTER 5

YOUR SPIRITUALITY & RECOVERY

In this chapter you will explore a fourth aspect of your personality. This aspect deals with your spirituality. Spirituality deals with your relationship to

A Higher Power

Nature

Humanity

It can have to do with religion, but this is not necessary. Many people who state that they don't believe in a Higher Power or God may still have a deep sense of

Spirituality

This could relate to a sense of awe, wonder, connectedness and responsibility for

The Universe

The Natural World

(including plants and animals)

Mankind

One can have this deep sense without ascribing to any religious code. On the other hand, you may define yourself as a member of an organized religion.

How would you describe your religion, if you have one?_____

_____

_____

Have you had a deep spiritual experience with:

Nature?_____

_____

Animals?_____

_____

Other persons?_____

_____

You are probably familiar with the Ten Commandments. If you were to write a list of rules on how people should live their lives, what would they be?

1. _____
2. _____
3. _____
4. _____
5. _____
6. _____
7. _____
8. _____
9. _____
10. _____

DEVIANCY AND SPIRITUALITY

In previous chapters you have seen how your physical body, your thoughts and your feelings have contributed to your deviancy. It may seem strange that your spirituality, your relationship to that which is sacred, good, moral and right could contribute to hurting others. It is very rare to find ministers, priests, rabbis, or other deeply religious individuals in prison for theft, assault or fraud. It is not at all uncommon for them to be in prison for

Sex Crimes

Just as people can misuse

> Food
>
> Money
>
> Sex
>
> Love

they can misuse RELIGION. They can be addicted to religion, if you define ADDICTION as "a compulsive and destructive relationship to a mood-altering substance or experience."

Father Leo Booth (1992), in <u>When God Becomes a Drug: Breaking the Chains of Religious Addiction and Abuse</u> states:

> I define religious addiction as using God, a church, or a belief system as
> an escape from reality, in an attempt to find or elevate a sense of self-
> worth or well-being. It is using God or religion as a fix. (p. 38)

You may already be feeling defensive. Are you feeling that a part of you that is powerful, good, positive, hopeful is being challenged?

> Yes   _____
>
> Maybe   _____
>
> No   _____

Your spiritual self can be a strong force for

> Recovery

but you must USE - not ABUSE it.

Remember, it did not keep you from OFFENDING - something must be wrong. For your spirituality to be a true force for good in your life, you must be honest in looking at how you use it. The very fact that you are in this trouble makes you at risk for misusing religion or spirituality.

PROGRESSION OF RELIGIOUS ADDICTION

EARLY STAGE	Ordinary religious or spiritual lifestyle — Using Bible to calm nerves — Praying before attending functions — Church/Bible becomes greater focal point — Black-and-white thinking increases — Excessive church-going/ Bible study — Using church/Bible/prayer to avoid problems — Missing family gatherings or work because of religious functions — Thinking only of church — Compulsively thinking about or quoting scripture — Preoccupation with church/ Bible study — Loss of control phase — Rationalization begins
MIDDLE STAGE	Increased use of church/Bible/ prayer to avoid problems — Thinking world/body evil — Church attendance bolstered by excuses crusades, proselytizing — Loss of other interests — Obsession with church/religion/ preacher — Sexuality is perceived as dirty — Excessive fasting/eating disorder — Efforts to control church-going fail — Isolation from people — Nonreligious family or friends judged or avoided — Loss of job — Secret irritation when religious practices discussed or criticized — Compulsive church attendance and scripture quoting — Obsessive praying, church-going, — Excessive financial contributions/tithing — Increasing dependence on religion — Feel guilt when missing church functions — Refuse to think critically/doubt/question information or authority — Unable to sensibly discuss religious issues — Brainwashing: family and friends — Grandiose and aggressive behavior — Conflict with school or work — Money problems — Preaching that sex is dirty
LATE STAGE	Radical deterioration of relationships — Sexual compulsive/obsessive behavior; sexual acting out — Physical and mental deterioration — Possibly seek therapy — Loss of family/friends — Unable to make decisions — Psychiatric assistance — Complete abandonment — Unreasonable resentment — Powerlessness — Lengthy crusades/mission work/ communes — "Messages" from God — Trances/stares — Isolation — Physical, mental, and emotional exhaustion — Hospitalization

Reprinted from Booth, L. (1992) <u>When God Becomes a Drug: Breaking the Chains of Religious Addiction and Abuse</u> with permission of Putnam Publishers.

According to Father Booth, there are definite stages of religious addiction. Read description and honestly analyze whether that behavior relates to you.

1. Thinking only in terms of black or white, right or wrong, good or bad, true or false.

   _____

   _____

   _____

2. Obsessive praying, going to services, quoting scripture, talking about religion.

   _____

   _____

   _____

3. Neglecting family, friends, community._____

   _____

   _____

   _____

4. Thinking the world, our physical body, sex is evil._____

   _____

   _____

   _____

5. Refusing to think, doubt or question._____

   _____

   _____

   _____

6.   Excessive fasting and compulsive overeating._____

_____

_____

_____

7.   Unrealistic financial contributions._____

_____

_____

_____

8.   Excessive judgmental attitudes._____

_____

_____

_____

9.   Isolation from others._____

_____

_____

_____

10.   Conflicts with education, science, therapy._____

_____

_____

_____

11.   Dramatic personality change resulting in a change in relationship with family, friends, employer._____

_____

_____

_____

12.   Unrealistic fears, guilt, shame, remorse._____

_____

_____

_____

13.   Cries for help; physical, mental, moral breakdown._____

_____

_____

_____

_____

_____

_____

14.   Did any members of your family show signs of religious addiction?_____

_____

_____

_____

_____

_____

_____

Father Booth (1992) suggests working on the following areas of recovery. Read each and consider carefully whether this is an area where you need work. Discuss how you might work on these issues.

1. Being open to criticism; not always having the answer. Learning to appreciate the "gray" areas of life. Not expecting yourself or others to be perfect._____

    _____

    _____

    _____

    _____

    _____

    _____

2. Seek to understand the broad concept of spirituality; understand how your spirituality dictates your responsibility to yourself and others._____

    _____

    _____

    _____

    _____

    _____

3. Appreciate the spirituality "gift" including your physical body, your sexuality, you as a person._____

    _____

    _____

    _____

    _____

    _____

4.   Consider the values of tolerance and personal forgiveness._____

_____

_____

_____

_____

_____

5.   Begin to talk about "buried feelings" - especially concerning guilt, fear, sexual abuse and shame issues._____

_____

_____

_____

_____

_____

SEX OFFENDERS AND RELIGIOUS ADDICTION

Sex offenders can misuse religion or spirituality in several ways.

1.   To justify your deviance

Did you

	Yes	No
* Believe that sex was "dirty"?	____	____
* Feel shameful over sex with another adult?	____	____
* Feel that female sexuality is sinful?	____	____
* Feel that sex with children is purer, less sinful?	____	____
* Feel that some women need to be punished?	____	____

Other ways you may have used your religious beliefs to justify your sexual deviance.

_____

_____

2.   To avoid dealing with sexual deviance

Did you

	Yes	No
* Use religious excuses to avoid parts of treatment?	___	___
* Claim that therapy prevents you from having time for your religion or visa-versa?	___	___
* Believe that God has forgiven you and that's all you need?	___	___
* Believe that you only committed your crime because you hadn't "found God"?	___	___
* Believe that you have been "born again" and thus don't need to do anything else?	___	___

SEEKING A SPIRITUAL PATH

"Only you can do it but
you can't do it alone."

Motto

The Dawn Unit

Central New Mexico

Correctional Facility

You can seek help outside of yourself and from sources of power inside yourself. Spirituality works when you can use it to

* Enhance your relationship to others
* Bring you peace
* Bring you courage
* Help you control panic, anger, hurting others, depression.

Are there people in your life or in books, movies, etc. Who have inspired you? List them and in what way they inspired you.

NAME / RELATIONSHIP   **INSPIRATION**

_____   _____

_____   _____

_____   _____

_____   _____

_____   _____

Is there a special place that inspires you, fills you with peace? Where?_____

_____

_____

_____

_____

Is there a song, poem or a saying that inspires you? What is it?_____

_____

_____

_____

_____

One of the ways that you can utilize your spirituality to assist you is through imagery. Take plenty of time to do the following. You may have dreams connected with this.

*Visualize your Shaman

A Shaman is a spiritual guide. Merlin was King Arthur's Shaman. It can be Christ, Buddha, a patron saint, a guardian angel, a totem animal, a mythical figure.

Draw a picture of your Shaman.

Describe a visit to your Shaman including how you would travel, where you would go, what you would ask your Shaman:_____

_____

_____

_____

_____

_____

_____

_____

_____

_____

_____

_____

What advice does your Shaman give you?_____

_____

_____

_____

_____

_____

_____

_____

Write a one sentence affirmation based on your Shaman's advice._____

_____

_____

_____

_____

_____

USING YOUR SPIRITUALITY TO ASSIST YOUR RECOVERY

There are a wide variety of ways that one can use one's spirituality to assist your recovery.

* First you will have to discover what your spirituality means to you.

* Second you will have to decide how to use it.

Today, millions of people around the world are utilizing their spirituality in their recovery through 12 - STEP PROGRAMS

> Alcoholics Anonymous
>
> Alanon
>
> ACOA Groups
>
> Narcotics Anonymous
>
> Gamblers Anonymous
>
> Fundamentalists Anonymous
>
> Emotions Anonymous
>
> Sexaholics Anonymous
>
> Sex Addicts Anonymous
>
> and many more

Individuals use 12 - Steps to:

> * Define and identify their higher power
>
> * Take responsibility for their lives
>
> * Make amends to others
>
> * Serve their communities

The 12 - Steps aren't something someone does once and that's done - THEY ARE A WAY OF LIFE.

THE 12 STEPS

Following are exercises to help you understand the 12 Steps. Doing the exercises is not the same as doing the Steps!! It is best to do the steps with the aid of a support group. The steps are fully explained in <u>The Big Book</u> of Alcoholics Anonymous.

STEP 1 deals with "Powerlessness and Unmanageability"

Part 1 - "We admitted that we are powerless over

alcohol

drugs

gambling

relationships

spending

eating

sex

You may say - "How can I ever recover if I'm powerless? However, the reverse is true. You can't recover as long as you believe that all you have to do is use your will power and you'll be fine.

"I can stop anytime I want to!"

<u>NO,</u> you can't!

Others may have told you - "You can stop if you <u>want</u> to." They are equally wrong.

You must learn how to control your behavior and the first step in learning is

To Admit You Don't Know The Answer.

Admitting that you are powerless is not the same as admitting you are weak - it's admitting you need

HELP

and that takes great strength.

Part 2 - "That our lives are unmanageable."

Look at all the ways your life has been messed up. How have the lives of others been harmed?

How many areas of your life have you harmed?_____

_____

_____

_____

_____

_____

_____

_____

_____

What are you addicted to?

_____

_____

_____

_____

_____

_____

_____

_____

_____

For each addiction, list the ways that addiction has placed your life or the quality of your life or the lives of others in jeopardy:

Addiction 1   Addiction 2   Addiction 3

_____   _____   _____

_____   _____   _____

_____   _____   _____

_____   _____   _____

_____   _____   _____

_____   _____   _____

(use additional pages if necessary)

How have you tried to control your addictions?

Addiction 1   Addiction 2   Addiction 3

_____   _____   _____

_____   _____   _____

_____   _____   _____

_____   _____   _____

_____   _____   _____

_____   _____   _____

(use additional pages if necessary)

How has your life been unmanageable?

Addiction 1	Addiction 2	Addiction 3
_____	_____	_____
_____	_____	_____
_____	_____	_____
_____	_____	_____
_____	_____	_____
_____	_____	_____

(use additional pages if necessary)

STEP 2 offers a promise of hope

"Came to believe that a Power greater than ourselves could restore us to sanity."

This power is not necessarily God. What is it in your life?_____

_____

_____

_____

_____

You may object to the word "insanity", but a definition of that word is "inability to manage one's own affairs and perform one's social duties."

Have you ever been: (check those that apply)

_____   Selfish

_____   Defiant

_____   Self - centered

_____   Frightened

_____   Self - deluded

_____   Self - seeking

_____   Self - pitying

Is your life the life of a Sane Person?

Step 3 involves an act of faith

"Made a decision to turn our will and our live's over to the care of God as we understand him."

You have used drugs, alcohol, sex, food, etc. to

Decrease pain

Ward off panic

Lessen fear

Control anger

and

many other purposes

However, this hasn't worked - it made things worse!

Let go - let God (or whatever your Higher Power may be.)

What can you give up right now?_____

_____

_____

_____

List, in order of difficulty, the things you need to "let go" of:

_____

_____

_____

_____

_____

_____

STEP 4 requires honesty

"Made a searching and fearless moral inventory of ourselves."

This is very difficult. No one wants to look at their Dark Side.

Can you honestly and truthfully

* Search - really dig into your life?
* Be fearless?
* Be moral?

In looking at your faults, you must admit the flaw and seek a better way. In the following exercises, admit the flaw and discuss how you can follow the positive path.

FLAW	**POSITIVE PATH**
False pride - refusing to admit weaknesses, being grandiose, staying in denial.	Humility - admitting you are human, accepting your flaws.

_____   _____

_____   _____

_____   _____

_____   _____

_____   _____

(Use more pages as necessary)

Perfectionism - refusing to accept the mistakes of yourself or others.

_____

_____

_____

_____

_____

Admitting Mistakes

_____

_____

_____

_____

_____

Being Phony

_____

_____

_____

_____

_____

Being Yourself

_____

_____

_____

_____

_____

Selfishness

_____

_____

_____

_____

Sharing

_____

_____

_____

_____

Impatience

_____

_____

_____

_____

_____

Patience

_____

_____

_____

_____

_____

Self-pity

_____

_____

_____

_____

_____

Feeling Good About Self

_____

_____

_____

_____

_____

Resentment

_____

_____

_____

_____

_____

Forgiveness and Understanding

_____

_____

_____

_____

_____

Intolerance

_____

_____

_____

_____

_____

Tolerance

_____

_____

_____

_____

_____

Alibis

_____

_____

_____

_____

_____

Being Honest

_____

_____

_____

_____

_____

Dishonest Thinking

_____

_____

_____

_____

Honest Thinking

_____

_____

_____

_____

Putting Things Off

_____

_____

_____

_____

Getting the Job Done

_____

_____

_____

_____

Guilt Feelings (using guilt as an excuse for victim standing)

_____

_____

_____

_____

Freedom from Guilt

_____

_____

_____

_____

Fear

_____

_____

_____

_____

Acceptance

_____

_____

_____

_____

Taking Things for Granted   Being Grateful

_____   _____

_____   _____

_____   _____

_____   _____

_____   _____

STEP 5 is a guide to reconciliation

"Admitted to God, to ourselves, and to another human being the exact nature of our wrongs."

This is a crucial step - do not fool yourself into thinking that admitting to yourself is the same as admitting to someone else.

In admitting these wrongdoings you

- own these behaviors

- take responsibility for them

- take control of them rather than having them control you.

You must put a great deal of effort into this.

* You must find the right person.

* You must find the right place.

* You must arrange for adequate time.

* You must write down what you wish to review.

Sex offenders may need to do their 5th Step with a clergyman if they need to admit to the <u>specifics</u> of additional crimes. Clergymen have the ability to keep <u>everything</u> they hear confidential. Even a friend may be legally bound to report past crimes, particularly if they involve child abuse of any kind.

In addition to selecting a person who can maintain confidentiality, you should select someone

> * You are comfortable with
>
> * Who understands the 12 Steps
>
> * Who is mature and wise
>
> * Who is trustworthy, respected and compassionate.

List persons you could ask to listen to your 5th Step:

_____

_____

_____

_____

Remember the discussion of SHAME and how one stuffs the wound full of anything that will conceal it? Doing the 5th STEP involves pulling the packing out.

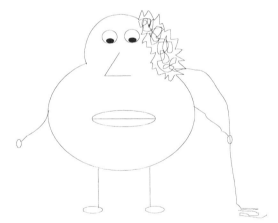

You will do much of this in your therapy but there may still be some details or specifics which you feel that you can't reveal because your therapist may be forced to report that to law enforcement. You will have to analyze your specific situation and decide what the risks are. However, you must get all the

Secrets

out or they will fester and keep the wound from healing.

In doing the 5th Step, keep these guidelines in mind:

* Tell your story - all your story.

* Use insight - why do you think you did these things.

* Let go of the past as you tell about it.

STEPS 6 & 7 are a process of surrender.

"We're entirely ready to have God remove all these defects of character."

"Humbly ask him to remove our shortcomings."

Are you really ready to give up your deviance? Your faults?

What are your fears about giving up your sexual deviance?_____

_____

_____

_____

_____

_____

What other character or personality flaws are you afraid to give up and why?

_____

_____

_____

_____

_____

_____

_____

What other addictions are you afraid to give up and why?_____

_____

_____

_____

_____

_____

_____

STEP 8 deals with restoring relationships.

"Make a list of all persons we had harmed and became willing to make amends to them."

Make a list of those persons. (Attach extra pages if necessary)

_____

_____

_____

_____

_____

_____

_____

_____

_____

_____

_____

_____

_____

STEP 9 is about making amends.

"Made direct amends to such people whenever possible except when to do so would injure them or others."

With some people you can directly apologize. These people must be

* Adults
* Able to work through their conflicts with you without denying their legitimate anger.
* Willing to work out their conflicts with you.
* It is probably best not to ask your victims for forgiveness except in a case where their therapist would recommend it.

Who are people you could apologize to?

_____

_____

_____

_____

_____

_____

_____

_____

_____

_____

There are some people you should not make an effort to contact. Who are they?

_____

_____

_____

_____

_____

_____

You may be able to make amends in an indirect or a symbolic manner. For each person you can't contact directly, make a list of other ways you might make amends.

PERSON   **ACTION**

_____   _____

                       _____

                       _____

                       _____

_____   _____

                       _____

                       _____

                       _____

_____   _____

                       _____

                       _____

                       _____

_____   _____

                       _____

                       _____

                       _____

_____   _____

_____

_____

_____

(Use more pages, if necessary)

Making amends must cost you something - your action should involve a significant investment which balances the harm you have done.

STEP 10 continues the process.

"Continued to take personal inventory and when we were wrong promptly admitted it."

This is where the 12 Steps become a way of life.

A business needs to take regular inventories or they will

* Overflow with unsalable merchandise.

* Have no idea what sells and what doesn't sell.

* Be unable to analyze how business is doing.

The 10th Step involves reworking Steps 1 - 9 on a daily basis.

In making a daily inventory, particularly analyze

> * Your thoughts and motivation
>
> * Your words
>
> * Your actions

There are a number of ways that people can camouflage their wrongs.

* The Drunkalog (Sexalog) - telling gripping horror tales about the past. Sex offenders may tell lurid tales of their crimes to sexually excite themselves and victimize others and they may do this in the name of honesty.

* Blanket Admission - making a broad, sweeping statement like "Everything in my life is messed up."

* Partial Admission - accept blame then transfer it to another. "Yes, I raped her but she wanted it."

A sex offender is discussing his crime in group. Give an example of how he would use:

The Sexalog_____

_____

_____

_____

_____

_____

_____

_____

_____

_____

_____

_____

The Blanket Admission_____

_____

_____

_____

_____

_____

_____

_____

_____

The Partial Admission_____

_____

_____

_____

_____

_____

_____

_____

_____

What small, daily flaws are you most likely to engage in?_____

_____

_____

_____

_____

_____

_____

_____

_____

An A.A. axiom says, "If somebody hurts us and we are sore, we are in the wrong also." Justifying being in a "victim stance" gives you a license to reoffend. What type of behavior puts you in a "victim stance"?

_____

_____

_____

_____

_____

_____

_____

_____

_____

How can you get out of a "victim stance"?_____

_____

_____

_____

_____

_____

_____

_____

_____

_____

Faithfully working the 10th Step will bring rewards.

> * Improved personal relationships.
>
> * Freedom from fear of "being found out."
>
> * Freedom from guilt.
>
> * Ability to help others.

> STEP 11 means maintaining a new way of life.
>
> > "Sought through prayer and meditation to improve our conscious contact with God, as we understand him, praying only for knowledge of his will for us and the power to carry that out."

This step requires that one gives up "self - will" - "Thou will, not mine, be done."

How can you best commune with your Higher Power?_____

_____

_____

_____

_____

_____

If you turned your life over to your Higher Power, what would you be afraid of?

_____

_____

_____

_____

_____

_____

_____

_____

_____

_____

STEP 12 means carrying the message to others.

"Having had a spiritual awakening as the result of these steps, we tried to carry this message to others."

You should remember that

* Spiritual awakening is an ongoing, never-ending process.

* Every person's spiritual awakening is unique.

Sharing with others can strengthen your recovery by

  * Letting you share yourself.

  * Allowing others to experience an awakening.

How can you help other sex offenders?

1._____

2._____

3._____

4._____

5._____

6._____

7._____

8._____

9._____

10._____

How can you help victims of sexual assault?

1._____

2._____

3._____

4._____

5._____

6._____

7._____

8._____

9._____

10._____

How can you help society deal with sexual assault?

1._____

2._____

3._____

4._____

5._____

6._____

7._____

8._____

9._____

10._____

There are many paths to

RECOVERY

While many people connect with

12 - Steps

there are other traditions as well.

One of these traditions comes from the teachings of

Native Americans

This tradition is known as

THE RECOVERY MEDICINE WHEEL

"All of life is a sacred medicine wheel. The old songs, the old teachings and the old ways are all lessons for us; lessons that point us in the right direction. If we follow that sacred path the medicine wheel will always turn inside of us."

Glen John/Navajo Medicine

Man, 1989 from

Coggins, Kip <u>The Recovery</u>

<u>Medicine Wheel: Alternative</u>

<u>Pathways to Healing</u>

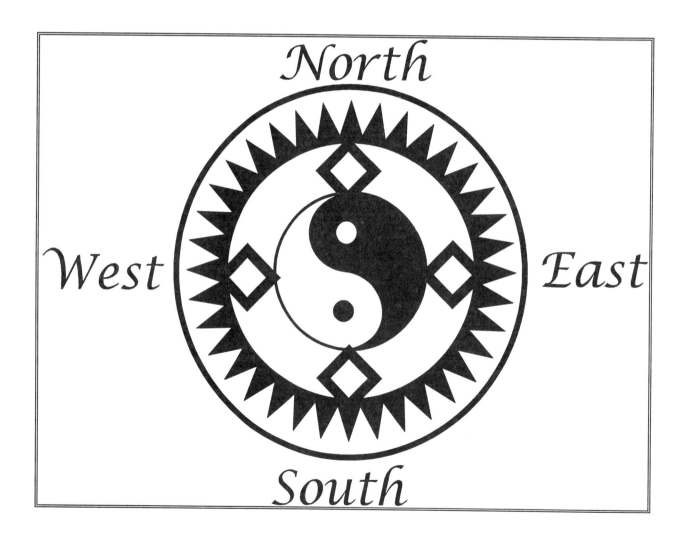

The Recovery Medicine Wheel addresses recovery in four realms

* The physical realm (North)

* The realm of knowledge and enlightenment (East)

* The spiritual realm (South)

* The realm of introspective thought (West)

(Coggins, 1990)

In following the recovery medicine wheel one chooses a starting point, usually North or West, and works clockwise around the wheel with each point being a lesson one must learn.

WALKING THE STEPS

Kip Coggins (1989) describes a number of steps towards recovery which correspond to the four directions and realms.

North: <u>The Physical Realm</u>

Step 1: Beginning today I will take good physical care of myself. (P.16)

Step 2: Beginning today I will regain balance in my life by developing an understanding of the important connection between the physical psychological, spiritual and emotional parts of my existence. (P.17)

Step 3: Beginning today I will stop inflicting pain (either physical or emotional) on others or myself. (P.18)

Step 4:   Beginning today I will come to an understanding that change is a process (I can't expect miracles overnight.)

East: The Realm of Knowledge and Enlightenment

Step 1:   Beginning today I will reawaken to all creation and all of the beauty that exists in the world around me." (P.21)

Step 2:   Beginning today I will release myself from a narrow view of life and begin to grow, learn, and gain new knowledge. (P.22)

Step 3:   Beginning today I will remember that I have a sacred right to live my life as I wish and the need to bring harmony and balance to my existence by respecting the rights of others. (P.23)

Step 4:   Beginning today I will work on understanding the changes I must make in order to achieve personal harmony, balance and freedom. (P.25)

South: The Spiritual Realm

Step 1:   Beginning today I will come to an understanding of my special relation to Mother Earth (release my pain to Mother Earth. (P.27)

Step 2:   Beginning today I will come to an understanding of my special relation to Father Sky. (P.28) By this the author is the opposing forces within us - aggression - gentleness.

Step 3:   Beginning today I will seek a greater understanding of my sacred connection to all of the universe. (P.29)

Step 4:   Beginning today I will reconnect with and nurture my own spirit. (P.30)

West: <u>The Realm of Introspective Thought</u>

Step 1:   Beginning today I will speak honestly with myself. (P.32)

Step 2:   Beginning today will look at my problems and my accomplishments with a willingness to commit myself to positive growth and change. (P.32)

Step 3:   Beginning today I will examine the ways in which I have tried to manipulate, control or manage the lives of others and to make a commitment to stop this behavior. (P.33)

Step 4:   Beginning today I will acknowledge that change in my life must begin with me. (P.35)

Write a recovery plan based on each step.

_____

_____

_____

_____

_____

_____

_____

_____

_____

_____

_____

_____

_____

_____

_____

You may have found it very difficult to fill in these plans. That's to be expected. If you chose to follow this Path, you would do it step-by-step and day-by-day, preferably with a support group.

The focus of this path is to find

Peace

Harmony

Balance

with

Yourself

All your fellow humans

All your fellow creatures

All of nature

"Within and around the earth,

within and around the hills,

within and around the mountains,

your authority returns to you."

CHAPTER 6

LOOKING AT FAMILIES

A healthy family creates a firm foundation for its members.

It provides

* A haven for rest, relaxation and rejuvenation.

* A source of nurturance and nourishment.

* A spiritual center to learn morals, ethics and relation to a Higher Power.

* A court in which justice and mercy both help teach the rules of society.

* A source of unqualified love.

YOUR FAMILY

Of course, this is an ideal family and very few families are ideal. However, healthy families do have certain characteristics. Evaluate your parental family on the following items (Evaluate the set of parents with whom you lived with for the longest period of time while you were under 15.)

	YES	?	NO
Each of your parents began their relationship as mature individuals.	___	___	___
Each of your parents came from functional families.	___	___	___
Your parents always discussed important decisions.	___	___	___

Your parents made decisions about
effective parenting as a couple.

    ___   ___   ___

Your parents established a parental unit and
supported each other.

    ___   ___   ___

Your parents set fair and consistent rules for
the children.

    ___   ___   ___

You parents had an active, supportive network
of friends.

    ___   ___   ___

Look at this evaluation. What conclusions do you reach about your parents?

_____

_____

_____

_____

_____

Patrick Carnes, Ph.D. (1989) in <u>Contrary to Love</u> describes the Circumplex Model (developed by David Olsen, Douglas Sprenkle, and Candyce Russel.) This model places families on two dimensions - adaptability and cohesion.

<u>Adaptability</u> - a family's capacity to organize and reorganize as the family grows and changes. This may be done in the following ways.

* Rigid - dictatorial style decision-making, limited negotiation and strictly defined roles and rules.

* Structured - combination of authoritarian and democratic leadership, very stable roles and rules.

* Flexible - democratic leadership, negotiated agreements, easily changing rules and roles.

* Chaotic - erratic, ineffective leadership, impulsive decisions, inconsistent rules, role reversals.

Families need to be able to change and grow in adaptability as the children grow.

How adaptable was your family? How would you describe their style (rigid - etc.)?

_____

_____

_____

_____

_____

_____

_____

_____

Cohesion - the degree of emotional support available in a family. Degrees of closeness include:

* Disengaged - family members are distant, maintain extreme separateness and little family loyalty.

* Separate - combination of emotional independence with some involvement and joint effort and occasional family loyalty.

145

* Connected - emphasizes emotional closeness, family loyalty, joint efforts while allowing for some individuality.

* Enmeshed - demand extreme family closeness, loyalty and allow for little individuality.

How would you rate your family on cohesion?_____

_____

_____

_____

ADAPTABILITY

COHESION		Rigid	Structured	Flexible	Chaotic
	Disengaged	1	2	3	4
	Separated	5	6	7	8
	Connected	9	10	11	12
	Enmeshed	13	14	15	16

Analyze each of the family types on the following dimensions. Use separate pages, if necessary.

Family Type	How Would This Type Handle Emotions?	How Would This Type Handle Discipline?	Functionality*
1. Rigid/Disengaged	_____	_____	_____
	_____	_____	
	_____	_____	
2. Structured/Disengaged	_____	_____	_____
	_____	_____	
	_____	_____	

146

3. Flexible/Disengaged _____ _____ _____
   _____ _____
   _____ _____

4. Chaotic/Disengaged _____ _____ _____
   _____ _____
   _____ _____

5. Rigid/Separated _____ _____ _____
   _____ _____
   _____ _____

6. Structured/Separated _____ _____ _____
   _____ _____
   _____ _____

7. Flexible/Separated _____ _____ _____
   _____ _____
   _____ _____

8. Chaotic/Separated _____ _____ _____
   _____ _____
   _____ _____

9. Rigid/Connected _____ _____ _____
   _____ _____
   _____ _____

10. Structured/Connected _____ _____ _____
    _____ _____
    _____ _____

11. Flexible/Connected _____ _____ _____
    _____ _____
    _____ _____

12. Chaotic/Connected _____ _____ _____
    _____ _____
    _____ _____

13. Rigid/Enmeshed   _____   _____   _____

                          _____   _____

                          _____   _____

14. Structured/Enmeshed   _____   _____   _____

                          _____   _____

                          _____   _____

15. Flexible/Enmeshed   _____   _____   _____

                          _____   _____

                          _____   _____

16. Chaotic/Enmeshed   _____   _____   _____

                          _____   _____

                          _____   _____

*Rank from: 1=Highly Functional   10=Highly Dysfunctional

How did your family handle discipline?_____

_____

_____

_____

How functional was your family? (Rate 1 - 10)_____

Which type best describes your family?_____How did your family handle

emotions?_____

_____

_____

_____

Which types would be associated with intrafamilial sexual assault?_____

Over 50% of sex offenders believed their families were rigid and disengaged.

DYSFUNCTIONAL FAMILIES

Families become dysfunctional for a number of reasons. They may have one or more of the following problems:

        Alcoholism

        Drug Abuse

        Mental Illness

        Physical Illness

        Abuse

        Other addictions

        and a variety of other problems

John Bradshaw (1989) states in <u>Healing the Shame That Binds You</u> that dysfunctional families tend to share certain rules which include

* Control - one must be in control at all times.

* Perfectionism - always be right in everything you do.

* Blame - whenever things don't turn out as planned, blame yourself or others.

* Denial of the Five Freedoms - denial of the power to perceive; to think and interpret; to feel; to want and choose; and the power to imagine.

* The No - Talk Rule - prohibit the full expression of any feeling, need or want.

* Don't Make Mistakes - mistakes reveal a flawed vulnerable self.

* Unreliability - don't expect reliability in relationships.

Rigid families with rigid rules follow rigid roles. They are not like a mobile which moves and balances in the breeze.

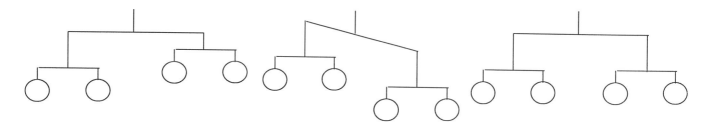

They are frozen and easily broken. Therefore members take on rigid roles.

ADDICT (or Identified Patient) - the person in the family who has the central addiction in the family system. This is the person that the family would identify as "the problem".

I hope this will get me through till the weekend.

THE ADDICT

I'm sorry but he's not coming into work today. He has the flu.

CHIEF ENABLER

CHIEF ENABLER - this is the person who must allow the addict to continue to abuse without experiencing the consequences of that abuse.

150

SUPERACHIEVER / FAMILY HERO

- this is the person who achieves outward success, wants to make family look good, super responsible.

SCAPEGOAT / DISTRACTER - this is the person who diverts attention away from main source of conflict and onto him / herself, openly hostile, defiant and acts out negative feelings.

QUIET / LOST ONE -
this person is never close to anyone, never a problem, withdrawn, little energy.

Bobby

MASCOT / COMEDIAN - this is the person who tries to laugh away pain, divert family attention with jokes.

Roles can change as family members change, grow up and leave. One family member may hold several roles, either concurrently or consecutively.

Were there rigid roles in your family? If so, who was the

Addict / Identified Patient   _____

Chief Enabler   _____

Superachiever / Family Hero   _____

Scapegoat / Distracter   _____

Quiet / Lost One   _____

Mascot / Comedian   _____

TOXIC SHAME - THE WOUND

Previously we described a way of thinking about toxic shame as a wound that is hidden but continues to fester. Healthy shame reminds us that we are human, have limits, make mistakes.

Toxic shame - "the all - pervasive sense that I am flawed and defective as a human being." (Bradshaw, 1989)

Toxic shame comes primarily from dysfunctional families and is passed down generation to generation. According to Bradshaw it is primarily caused by:

* "Identification with shame - based models" being raised by parents who harbored toxic shame.
* "Trauma of abandonment" - physical psychological neglect, abuse, parental absence.
* "Interconnection and magnification of visual memories of scenes." - vivid memories of shaming experiences.

Toxic shame can also come from:

Peers -   who ridicule anyone they see as different.

Schools -   that ridicule their students.

Religion -   that may make people feel they are sinners or that their natural impulses are sinful.

Culture -   that discriminates against minorities or those who are "different".

Do you feel that you suffer from Toxic Shame?

Do you often feel:

	Yes	No
* Exposed or vulnerable	_____	_____
* Embarrassed by who you are	_____	_____
* Shy	_____	_____
* Flawed	_____	_____
* Isolated and alone	_____	_____

Where do you think those feelings came from? Your family_____

_____

_____

_____

Your peers_____

_____

_____

Your school_____

_____

_____

Your religion_____

_____

_____

Your culture_____

_____

_____

ADULT CHILDREN OF DYSFUNCTIONAL FAMILIES

Children who are raised in dysfunctional families don't leave home and suddenly become healthy humans. They carry the scars of their experiences and develop many characteristics.

They may:

* Attempt to stay in control at all times.

* Ignore their accomplishments.

* Seek constant external affirmation.

* Be super responsible or super irresponsible.

* Act perfectionistically.

* Act as constant caretakers.

* Have low self - esteem.

Which characteristics describe you?_____

_____

_____

_____

_____

_____

_____

_____

The degree to which individuals may have been harmed by growing up in a dysfunctional family depends on a number of situations.

* The degree to which the parent focuses on the child's need rather than the needs of the addict, addiction or dysfunction.

* Whether one or both parents are dysfunctional

* The more functional parent's response to the dysfunction

* Stage of the addiction or severity of dysfunction

* When in child's development does the dysfunction occur

* Presence of other supportive family members or substitutes (Teddy Bear person)

* Child's basic temperament

* Birth order

(Middleton-Moz and Dwinnell, 1986)

What factors made your situations better or worse?_____

_____

_____

_____

_____

_____

_____

DEFENDING AGAINST THE PAIN

People use all types of defenses against dealing with the pain of their past.

Repression -   bury the incident/s and emotion/s that go with it.

Denial -   refuse to admit what is happening or happened in the past.

Projection -   attribute your problems, feelings to others.

Dissociation -   numbing which can produce amnesia.

Displacement -   associating an emotion with a source different than the true one.

Identification -   identifies with the victimizer so that one no longer feels helpless or humiliated.

Conversion -   convert thoughts and feelings into different ones.

Acting - out -   expressing emotion through angry or antisocial behavior.

Do any of these defenses fit you?

_____

_____

_____

_____

_____

_____

_____

_____

_____

_____

_____

_____

Look at your own relationships. People are often drawn to each other for the wrong reasons. They come together out of their weaknesses rather than their strengths. A man with little self-confidence may select a woman who has major problems. Sometimes couples form in an attempt to relive and fix old traumas. A woman whose father was alcoholic may grow up believing that if she had only done the right thing, her father would have stopped drinking. Consequently, she marries alcoholics believing she can "fix" them. this rare, if ever, works. Did you get into codependent relationships or did others get into codependent relationships with you?_____

_____

_____

_____

_____

_____

CHAPTER 7

PLANNING FOR YOUR RECOVERY

Your recovery will depend on how well you can apply what you have learned in treatment to your real life.

You will need to make major changes in your lifestyle.

You will need to plan for your new life very carefully.

Rather than keep it open ended, you should set a realistic date by which you will complete your recovery plan. Leave your self enough time to be complete in all your recovery tasks but not so far off that you loose your momentum.

_____

Goal Date

Your goal date may seem far away but it's sooner than it seems. You should complete the plans in this chapter even though your release date is fairly remote so that you will learn the process.

YOUR SUPPORT SYSTEM

One of the most important factors in your Recovery will be an active support system. You need to select adults who will:

* Provide emotional support.

* Be able to talk openly with you about your sexual deviancy.

* Be assertive enough to confront you if you are in your cycle.

* Be able to report you to your therapist, your Community Corrections Office or law enforcement if they feel you are about to reoffend.

* Be capable of handling the criticism of others for befriending you.

* Be someone whom you feel that you could be comfortable talking with about anything.

NAME	ADDRESS	PHONE

NAME	ADDRESS	PHONE

Most of your support system should live close enough to you so that you can readily seek their support.

Where will you live when you are released?_____

Contact a member of your support system and have them send you the want ads from recent back issues of the newspapers in that area. By studying these, you will be able to get a feel for the housing and employment opportunities.

YOUR THERAPY

Your therapy is your first priority.

Who will be your therapist? This person must have expertise in treating sexual deviancy, utilize group therapy and be thoroughly familiar with Relapse Prevention.

_____   _____

          Name   Location

You may need to attend self - help groups to help you cope with other addictions. List the ones you need to attend below.

_____

_____

_____

_____

_____

_____

With the help of your support system, identify the location and meeting times of these groups.

NAME	LOCATION	MEETING TIME
_____	_____	_____
_____	_____	_____
_____	_____	_____
_____	_____	_____
_____	_____	_____
_____	_____	_____
_____	_____	_____
_____	_____	_____
_____	_____	_____

Is there any other type of treatment you need, such as medication? Where will you get that?

_____   _____
Name   Location

YOUR JOB

What type of a job or jobs would you like to get?

_____   _____

_____   _____

_____   _____

_____   _____

Looking at the want - ads, copy three ads relating to the jobs you would like to get.

_____

    Job 1

_____

    Job 2

_____

Job 3

_____
_____
_____
_____
_____
_____
_____
_____
_____
_____
_____

How much money can you realistically expect to earn?

$_____Per_____

In order to find a job, you will need a resume. You should go to the library and get a book on doing a resume.

_____   _____

        Name of book   Author

Write a resume and attach a copy.

On the job application there may be a question like "Have you ever been convicted of a felony?". How will you respond to this?_____

_____

_____

_____

_____

_____

_____

_____

_____

_____

_____

What types of jobs would be high risk situations?

_____

_____

_____

_____

_____

_____

_____

_____

_____

_____

What will you tell your employer about your situation?_____

_____

_____

_____

_____

_____

_____

YOUR HOUSING

Where will you live? You may already have a home that you can return to. Where will you go on the day you are released from prison or work release?

_____   _____

Whose Home   Address

How long would you live there?_____

If you need to establish your own home, complete the following.

How much do you realistically think you can afford to pay?_____
(Have you figured utilities, phone, etc.?)

Copy ads of places that would be suitable.

_____   _____

_____   _____

_____   _____

_____   _____

_____   _____

_____   _____

_____   _____

_____   _____

What types of housing would be high risk situations?

_____

_____

_____

_____

_____

_____

_____

In some states there is a process called Public Notification in which neighbors, sometimes entire communities, could be notified of your name, crime and address. What would you do if the community was notified of your presence?_____

_____

_____

_____

_____

_____

_____

_____

_____

_____

_____

_____

_____

_____

_____

YOUR TRANSPORTATION

Do you have a car?_____

Is it in good running condition?_____

Will you need a car?_____

Have you explored other types of transportation? List the initial and ongoing expense of each. You may need to have one of your support members supply you with some of this information.

TYPE	INITIAL COST	UPKEEP	ADVANTAGES	DISADVANTAGES
Motorcycle	_____	_____	_____	_____
	_____	_____	_____	_____
	_____	_____	_____	_____
	_____	_____	_____	_____

Bus or Pass   _____   _____   _____   _____

                 _____   _____   _____   _____

                 _____   _____   _____   _____

                 _____   _____   _____   _____

Bicycle   _____   _____   _____   _____

                 _____   _____   _____   _____

                 _____   _____   _____   _____

                 _____   _____   _____   _____

Car Pool   _____   _____   _____   _____

                 _____   _____   _____   _____

                 _____   _____   _____   _____

                 _____   _____   _____   _____

Other   _____   _____   _____   _____

                 _____   _____   _____   _____

                 _____   _____   _____   _____

If you decide that you definitely need a car, how will you get it and what will it cost? Copy three ads of cars you feel you will be able to afford.

_____   _____

_____   _____

_____   _____

_____   _____

_____   _____

_____   _____

_____   _____

_____

_____

_____

_____

_____

_____

_____

_____

What will it cost to maintain that car?

License _____

Gas/oil per month _____

Insurance per year _____

Routine maintenance per month _____

Emergency repairs per year _____

OTHER NEEDS AND EXPENSES

There are many expenses in setting up your new life. You need to know how much these will cost and where you can get them.

Utilities (if not included in rent) _____

(Gas, electricity, water, sewage, garbage) *Hook-up*

_____

Monthly Bill

Phone (if you need one)   _____

Hook-up

_____

Monthly Bill

Clothing:

Needed Items   Cost

_____   _____

_____   _____

_____   _____

_____   _____

_____   _____

_____   _____

_____   _____

_____   _____

Total=_____

Where are some places where you can get inexpensive or free clothing?

_____

_____

_____

_____

Furniture:

Needed Items	Cost
_____	_____
_____	_____
_____	_____
_____	_____
_____	_____
_____	_____
_____	_____
_____	_____

Total = _____

Where are some places where you can acquire these at a discount?_____

_____

_____

_____

Housewares (Dishes, pots and pans, bedding, cleaning materials, etc.):

Needed Items	Cost
_____	_____
_____	_____
_____	_____
_____	_____
_____	_____
_____	_____
_____	_____

Total = _____

Where are some places where you can get these at a discount?_____

_____

_____

_____

_____

Other items you feel you will need:

Needed Items	Cost
_____	_____
_____	_____
_____	_____
_____	_____
_____	_____
_____	_____
_____	_____
_____	_____

Total =_____

Where are some places where you can get these at a discount?_____

_____

_____

_____

_____

Many people enjoy sharing their life with a pet. If you want to have a pet, can you afford one, keep one with your housing arrangement, afford to give it quality care? If you wish to keep a pet, complete the following: (List only animals that you feel you would have a reasonable chance of being able to keep.)

Type	Initial Cost	Supply Cost	Feed Per Week	Other Expenses
_____	_____	_____	_____	_____
_____	_____	_____	_____	_____
_____	_____	_____	_____	_____
_____	_____	_____	_____	_____
_____	_____	_____	_____	_____
_____	_____	_____	_____	_____
_____	_____	_____	_____	_____
_____	_____	_____	_____	_____
_____	_____	_____	_____	_____

YOUR FREE TIME

Previously you analyzed some ways you can spend your free time. List below what you plan to do, where you will do it and the expense involved.

WHAT	WHERE	HOW MUCH
_____	_____	_____
_____	_____	_____
_____	_____	_____
_____	_____	_____
_____	_____	_____
_____	_____	_____

Are there any clubs or organizations that you would like to attend?

_____   _____

NAME   LOCATION

YOUR LEGAL OBLIGATIONS

You may still have obligations relating to your crime when you are released.

Do you have community supervision?_____What will you be required to do?

_____

_____

_____

_____

_____

_____

Do you have to pay restitution?_____How much?_____

To whom?_____

_____

_____

Do you have special court ordered requirements?_____What are they?

_____

_____

_____

_____

_____

_____

_____

Will you have to register as a sex offender?_____Where?_____

How do you feel about that?_____

_____

_____

_____

_____

_____

_____

If any of these will be a special problem, discuss that here_____

_____

_____

_____

_____

_____

_____

_____

_____

FINDING FRIENDS

Do you have friends, other than your support team, whom you believe will be your friend when you get out?

NAME

Describe what type of friendship it is (drinking buddies, fishing buddies)

_____	_____
_____	_____
_____	_____
_____	_____
_____	_____
_____	_____
_____	_____
_____	_____
_____	_____
_____	_____

Go back and mark out the name of any friend who would not help you in your recovery. Consider beginning a correspondence with those that would assist you in your recovery - even if it's just a note to keep in touch.

List places where you might be able to meet appropriate friends. Have a support team person help you find out about <u>non - alcoholic</u> social clubs, dance clubs, living units, hobby clubs.

Place	**Address**
_____	_____
_____	_____
_____	_____
_____	_____
_____	_____
_____	_____
_____	_____
_____	_____
_____	_____
_____	_____
_____	_____
_____	_____
_____	_____
_____	_____

CONCLUSION

You have come to the end of this workbook. Hopefully you have learned about your deviance and your recovery. Try to summarize some of this information in some simple rules for your life.

In order to live a

healthy, productive life

I MUST NOT   **I MUST**

1. _____   _____

2. _____   _____

3. _____   _____

4. _____   _____

5. _____   _____

Congratulations! By the time you complete this workbook, you have given lots of thought to your deviance and your recovery. You will need to be open and honest in the rest of your treatment. Every day you will need to apply what you have learned. You will need to turn to others for assistance.

Recovery is a journey.

Best of luck!

REFERENCES

(1976) <u>Alcoholics Anonymous</u>
New York: Alcoholics Anonymous.

Ardell, D.B. (1982) <u>Planning For Wellness</u>
Dubuque, IA: Kendall/Hunt.

Bradshaw, J. (1989) <u>Healing The Shame That Binds You</u>
Pompano Beach, FL: Health Communications.

Booth, L. (1992) <u>When God Becomes a Drug: Breaking the Chains of Religious</u>
<u>Addiction and Abuse</u>, Torrence, CA: Jeremy P. Tarcher, Inc.

Carnes, P. (1989) <u>Contrary To Love: Helping the Sexual Addict</u>
Minneapolis, MN: CompCare.

Cellini, H.R. (1990) <u>Can You Change?</u>
Albuquerque, NM: TRI Corp.

Coggins, K. (1990) <u>Alternative Pathways to Healing: Recovery Medicine Wheel</u>
Deerfield Beach, FL: Health Communications.

Gelatt, H.B., Varenhorst, B. and Carey, R. (1972) <u>Deciding</u>
New York City: College Entrance Examination Board.

Middleton-Moz, J. and Dwinnell, L. (1986) <u>After The Tears</u>
Deerfield Beach, FL: Health Communications.

Schwartz, B.K. and Cellini, H. (1995) <u>The Sex Offender: Corrections, treatment</u>
<u>and Legal Practice</u>, Kingston, NJ: Civic Research Institute.

Order Form

Shipping Address:

Name _____
Agency _____
Department _____
City _____ State_____ Zip_____
Phone _____Fax _____

Billing Address (if different from shipping address):

Name _____
Agency _____
Department _____
City_____ State_____ Zip_____
Phone _____Fax _____

YOUR PURCHASE ORDER NUMBER:

Qty	Title	Unit Price	Total Cost
	The Sex Offender: 3 Volume Set	$270.50[1]	
	The Sexual Predator	$98.95[1]	
	Facing the Shadow[2]		

Shipping[3]	
Subtotal	
Non-exempt NY and NJ residents add sales tax	
Total	

Make checks payable to:
Civic Research Institute, Inc.
US Funds only. Prices subject to change.

[1] Price includes shipping and handling.
[2] See price list below for unit pricing on Facing the Shadow.
[3] See price list below for shipping on Facing the Shadow.

Units		Discount	Price Per Copy	Shpg/Hdlg Per Copy
0	1	0%	$24.95	$5.95
2	4	10%	$22.46	$4.49
5	9	20%	$19.96	$3.99
10	19	25%	$18.71	$2.81
20	49	30%	$17.47	$2.10
50	99	40%	$14.97	$1.50
100	+	Call for price		

Mail order form to:
Civic Research Institute, Inc.
P.O. Box 585
Kingston, NJ 08528
Or fax your order:
609-683-7291

Order Form

Shipping Address:

Name _____
Agency _____
Department _____
City _____ State_____ Zip_____
Phone _____ Fax _____

Billing Address (if different from shipping address):

Name _____
Agency _____
Department _____
City_____ State_____ Zip_____
Phone _____ Fax _____

YOUR PURCHASE ORDER NUMBER:

Qty	Title	Unit Price	Total Cost
	The Sex Offender: 3 Volume Set	$270.50[1]	
	The Sexual Predator	$98.95[1]	
	Facing the Shadow[2]		

Shipping[3]	
Subtotal	
Non-exempt NY and NJ residents add sales tax	
Total	

Make checks payable to:
Civic Research Institute, Inc.
US Funds only. Prices subject to change.

[1] Price includes shipping and handling.
[2] See price list below for unit pricing on Facing the Shadow.
[3] See price list below for shipping on Facing the Shadow.

Units		Discount	Price Per Copy	Shpg/Hdlg Per Copy
0	1	0%	$24.95	$5.95
2	4	10%	$22.46	$4.49
5	9	20%	$19.96	$3.99
10	19	25%	$18.71	$2.81
20	49	30%	$17.47	$2.10
50	99	40%	$14.97	$1.50
100	+	Call for price		

Mail order form to:
Civic Research Institute, Inc.
P.O. Box 585
Kingston, NJ 08528
Or fax your order:
609-683-7291